CROSS-CULTURAL TRANSITION HANDBOOK

A Training Manual for Students International

This Book Belongs To:

_____

By Stephen W. Jones

I AM INTERCULTURAL
An Imprint of Excegent Communication

Table of Contents

Students International

Established in 1993, Students International (SI) is a nondenominational, Christian ministry organization. SI is a qualified 501(c)(3) charity and has missionaries serving in four countries throughout the world. The International Service Center, located in Visalia, California, provides leadership, supervision and support service in the areas of funds development, human resources, information technology, finance and administration, ministry and program development, and marketing.

Our Ministry Style

Our overall ministry style is relational and is therefore centered around the long term presence of our staff missionaries within the communities where we have a presence. This may be challenging for short term participants who expect to see immediate "results" in evangelism and project completion. Over time, however, not only do we see projects completed, we also see staff, participants and the poor transformed into the likeness of Christ and discover their true calling.

The most common objectives for short-term mission outreaches are to broaden our perspective of the world and our responsibility to it, deepen our relationship with the Lord, and share the Gospel with others in need. We also intentionally strive to accomplish other goals such as:

- Enable outreach participants and the poor to discover how God can use them in their occupation or area of interest.

- Provide outreach participants and the poor the opportunity to be a part of ongoing ministry and not just a short outreach where follow up is difficult. (This is one benefit of partnering long-term missionaries with short-term outreach participants.)

- Help outreach participants and the poor understand the value of meeting real needs and building personal relationships through which the Gospel can be shared.

Our Mission

Our mission is:

Bringing students and the poor together cross-culturally
to encounter God, share the Good News, disciple and serve others in
occupational ministries.

Our Vision

Our vision is:

Seeing students and the poor transformed into the likeness of Christ and
discover their true calling.

Introduction:
Why This Handbook?

Every year, millions of people are engaged in cultural transition. Study abroad students and facilitators, international students, missionaries, Peace Corps Volunteers, global service learners, international businesspeople and business travelers, aid and development workers, military members, and trailing spouses and third-culture kids are all undergoing cross-cultural transitions every day.

Unfortunately, many people are underprepared for the disruptions caused by these transitions, and are unable to make the most of their experiences. Many people have a vague sense that they have not gotten all they could out of their cultural exchange, and some are left with a lasting inability to integrate valuable lessons into their life.

The bad: The results of poor preparation for cultural transition can be stark. Lack of proper reintegration can result in lost productivity, unplanned vocational changes, and broken relationships. Cultural transitions are so potentially disruptive that mental illness can result from cultural transitions that are not fully or properly processed.

The good: When sojourners effectively prepare for and engage in cultural transitions, the results can be phenomenally good. Broadened perspectives, increased creative capacity, and expanded networks can result from well-managed cultural transitions.

Why I Wrote this Handbook

I have been personally involved in cultural transitions since the 1980s, when I was growing up as the son of a naval officer. The first transition I remember was from Virginia to Texas. I began kindergarten there, and Texas does a great job of instilling the love of the place in young children. But after two years in Texas public schools, we were headed off to Japan. I remember looking at books from the library with my mom and sister and being not only bewildered but terrified about this strange and faraway place.

Japan ended up being a wonderful place to live, but between the death of my grandfather shortly after we moved, my dad's long deployments with Desert Shield and Desert Storm, and the Mt. Pinatubo eruption in the Philippines, I was ready to return to the US in fourth grade.

Coming back to the US was good but very hard. We lived in southern California for about nine months and then headed to Kansas. In a situation to which many military brats and third culture kids can relate, I was in three different schools my fourth-grade year, each in vastly different places.

It wasn't until I was working on my master's degree that I really discovered the principles of culture shock, reentry, and what the third-culture kid is. I repeatedly called my sister with new insights: "I just found out why we were so messed up!"

After studying in Mexico for six months as part of a global service-learning program in college, I decided to go into education. In the last decade, I have been working with college students in various stages of cultural transition as well. I have worked with students preparing to study in Asia, Europe, Latin America, and Africa. I have traveled with and been responsible for students in Africa and Latin America, as well as in various regions in the US, including on an Indian Reservation in South Dakota, in the Deep South, and in the Pacific Northwest.

One of the most unfortunate things I have observed is how few people are well prepared for cross-cultural transitions. I have seen, in my own students, the difference in success between students who are well prepared and those who aren't. I have also seen tremendous differences between those who recognize the realities of culture shock and reentry and those who are unaware of the effects of these phenomena. Without a doubt, those who understand why culture shock happens and how to deal with it are more successful in the long run.

Yet there are too many schools, businesses, and organizations that don't take seriously how disruptive culture shock can be. Even Christian organizations, with venerable histories of missions work around the world are not immune from this weakness. I recall giving a reentry training for first term missionaries in the first months of their furlough who asked "why couldn't we have been told all this six months ago?" Unfortunately, there is no good reason – this handbook does not present new information. Indeed, much more noted authors than myself[1] have written about far more than appears in this particular volume. However, this handbook has been written with four distinct purposes that may help to close the gap between the knowledge that exists in the literature and the experience of individuals such as those missionaries who were so frustrated with the inadequate preparation they received.

1. The first, and most immediate, is to enable Students International staff and participants who are actually traveling to understand what they can expect and how to cope with the disorientation caused by cross-cultural transitions.

2. The second purpose is to enable those responsible for travelers, including Students International domestic and international staff, to understand the seriousness of the cross-cultural transition so they can make appropriate decisions about supporting these individuals.

---

1 see, for example, Hiebert, Anthropological Insights for Missionaries; Paige, "On the Nature of Intercultural Experiences and Intercultural Education Chapter 1"; Ward, Bochner, and Furnham, Psychology Culture Shock - Ed2; Storti, The Art of Coming Home; Storti, The Art of Crossing Cultures; Pollock and Van Reken, Third Culture Kids.

3. The third purpose is to enable supporters of travelers, such as parents, friends, and loved ones, to understand what the traveler is experiencing so they can provide better support.

4. The final purpose is to specifically address the needs of Christians in the transition process.

Do We Really Need This?

For experienced travelers and mission trip facilitators, it can be easy to assume that you already know everything you need to about transitioning across cultures. Indeed, it is possible that your unique combination of training, education, and experience has prepared you not only to be excellent at transitioning across cultures yourself, but also to be very skilled at helping others to transition. If that is the case, though, I suspect that you will readily see the utility of a new tool in your kit for helping others to transition. My own experience is that I have yet to find a tool that I am satisfied with – the very reason I wrote this handbook for you. Of course, you will need to supplement this tool with others, and a number of references will be made throughout the course of the handbook.

What to Expect in this Book

This short book is intended to enable Students International sojourners, the people responsible for them, and those who love them to better prepare for, process, and reintegrate from cultural transitions. This handbook is intentionally concise, designed to provide the basic principles for successful intercultural exchanges, relationships, and transitions.

To accomplish this goal, each chapter of this book contains a mixture of intercultural theory and examples. Finally, readers can expect to find specific guidelines for intercultural engagement and practical tips on how to make the most of applying the theory.

Bolded words can be found in the glossary for clarification.

How to Use this Book

The handbook is intended to be used at specific intervals as you prepare to travel, while you are in the midst of your sojourn, and (if appropriate) when you return from your journey. In each of these three distinct time periods, the transition may be experienced differently. The book will be most effective if you read it as you Prepare to go (**Prepare**), while you are away from home in your Sojourn location (**Sojourn**), and again as you Return (**Return**).

As suggested by Clayton[2], reflection can be used to generate, deepen, and document learning. Given the power of reflective practice to shape not only your thinking but the experience itself, this handbook contains questions and exercises that allow you to capture your thoughts and reflections on the book's content while you are in each of these time periods.

To assist you, the book provides blank sections for your notes as you respond to the questions and exercises. For additional room to write, we have provided note pages at the end of the book. As you move through your sojourn experience, take the time to read and reflect on the text and your prior notes, as they will help you recognize the changes in your perceptions as you progress through these experiences.

INTRODUCTION REFLECTION

1. If applicable, when have you transitioned across cultures before?

2. Have you seen other people transition across cultures before?

---

2 Clayton, "Generating, Deepening, and Documenting Learning: The Power of Critical Reflection in Applied Learning."

3. If you have transitioned across cultures or have observed others transition across cultures, what do you think was helpful in your/their experience or might have caused your/their experience to be more successful?

4. If you are responsible for helping others to transition across cultures, what do you want to know about so that you can help them to be more effective in their transitions?

5. The author writes about events in his life that influenced why he wrote the book. Have you encountered events in your life that might have caused you to consider writing a book about transitioning across cultures?

Additional Notes

Chapter One:
All Too Real

A decision had to be made…the Peace Corps had been sent out of the country and most of the missionaries had left – even the ones who wanted to stay. But my six American students and the intern alumna facilitating their experience were content. The coup d'état had been quick, and even though they had heard the gunfire as the coup happened they were unshaken in their commitment to stay in-country.

We had been able to remove them from the capital – they were originally supposed to be two hours south anyway, but scheduling never seems to be quite what you expect. Down in the south of the country, the team of American college students was excelling in the local language to a degree I had never seen before. They were the best adjusted team of students I had ever seen, and, two months into their six month sojourn, they were on the verge of having some of the most impactful ministry to have come out of a team like this.

The hosts, ever gracious members of the national evangelical denomination which ran the program in-country, expressed confidence in the safety of the team. The conflict in the capital seemed to be minimal now, and the fighting in the north of the country was far enough away that it was not a major concern. And yet…

The sporadic closing and opening of the borders and the airport increased the uncertainty about what-ifs. The college administration, with no expertise on the matter, were for the moment satisfied to look to me to make the decision. However, I was confident that that situation would change. My concerns about removing the students from the country were multitudinous: How do I minimize the impact on the national church? How do the students complete their program requirements? What are the logistically feasible options? And, not least, if the students come back to the US, what does high-quality member care[3] look like?

I tried multiple combinations of options – perhaps they could cross the land border into a neighboring country and wait with missionaries there. The missionaries were willing but the national church rejected this because of possible dangers at the border crossing. A second option was to leave them in place and pray that the security situation would remain acceptable. This was actually my preferred option, and was consistent with the advice we were getting from

---

3 O'Donnell, *Doing Member Care Well.*

the embassy. But once the Peace Corps was removed I knew it was just a matter of time until the administration made the call to remove the students. It was as though there was a loaded gun in my hand, and I realized that it would either go off because the administration reached over to pull the trigger, regardless of where the gun was pointing, or I could take careful aim and pull the trigger myself.

It was thus that I decided to recall the students, over their significant protestations. I saw a window of time where I could act unhindered to provide them with what support could be offered and allow me to give them a fighting chance at a healthy transition. And so, they left the country they had planned to call home for another four months and returned to the US – but not to home.

Rather than bring them back to the Midwest college where they studied, I arranged for them to stay at a missionary training center in central Florida for the remaining two months of the Spring semester. They arrived in Orlando and we stayed a couple of nights at a hotel to provide a neutral location as they began processing their reentry to the US. And they began to let me know what they thought. They were angry to be back in the US. They had felt safe in-country and didn't see any reason to leave. They were mad, too, about the loss of the debrief that was supposed to have happened in Paris that was made impossible by the quick trip back.

The second day we met with a counselor from another mission agency who did not observe in them any signs of trauma beyond the frustration of having been called out early. And so, we made the trek to the mission training center – a simulated developing world village they had stayed at for a few weeks before heading out to their on-site placement. They knew most of the staff, and they settled in for a couple of months of class and transition.

By the third week, the training institute students began to notice that my students were increasingly difficult to get along with. Far from being the care-free easygoing team with an exciting experience that they had first seemed to be, they were moody and unpleasant. Finally, the training institute students addressed the institute director about this – why were these students – the ones who had been "missionaries" in a developing world country for two months – so far from demonstrating the fruit of the Spirit? Why were they so difficult to like? Why did they only care about themselves and complain?

And then, God worked the miracle that was needed. The institute director had himself been a missionary who had been removed from a developing world country as a result of a coup d'état. In fact, he and his wife had gone through three coups. Once, they stayed. Once, they chose to leave. And once, they chose to stay but were forced by their organization to leave. And so, he helped his students to see that the process my students were going through was a process that he himself had gone through. He suggested to his students that if my students had not been able to relocate to Florida that they would very likely be enacting this whole ugly process with their families, potentially scarring those relationships permanently. Struck by this, his students made the bold decision to trust Christ and to love my students – "better us than their families" they said.

As the second month drew to a close, we had a debrief and celebrated the end of their time in Florida with a trip to Disney. The Eiffel tower at Epcot is a poor replacement for the real one. One of my students asked the barista at the Epcot Paris bakery/coffee shop how to get to the Eiffel tower (intending the one at Epcot), to which the barista stingingly replied "go to Paris!" But together we implanted a memory of the end of the trip that will help them to remember their experience for decades to come whenever they see the Disney castle, the Epcot ball, or the mouse-ears.

And yet, this was not the end. Although I had moved on from the college by the next fall, I returned to teach a semester-long one credit reentry and debrief class for that same group. We met once a week for the full semester. Even though that class ended more than eight months after they returned from their host country, there continued to be fresh items brought up for processing their experience through that whole semester.

It is impossible to know answers to the many what-ifs. What if we had left the students in-country? What if they had gone straight home instead of to Florida? What if the institute director hadn't known what the students' experience was like?

What we can know is that these students lived through a complex situation that required rapid decision-making about how to facilitate a transition across cultures. Hopefully you will not face a situation like this (or one of the far worse situations that teams and individuals sometimes encounter). Yet the principles that guided my decision making in this situation are the same principles that guide my decision making for the much more 'normal' transitions that most of my students experience. It is these principles that follow in the remainder of the handbook, laid out as "Big Ideas." As you go, you can reflect not only on your own experience, but also on how you might apply the insights of each Big Idea to this all-too-real situation.

CHAPTER ONE REFLECTION

1. Why did the author decide to have the students go to a third location when they were removed from their host country?

2. What was the purpose of the visit to Disney World?

3. Have you ever undergone an unexpected transition? If so, describe it.

4. If yes to #3, what helped you to process your transition?

5. What principles do you think should guide a person's cross-cultural transition process, regardless of how intense it is?

Additional Notes

Chapter Two:
What Is Culture?

Big Idea #1:
Culture is the way people do life together

As early as the 1960's, more than 160 definitions for culture had been identified.[4] For the purpose of this book, we are really interested in exploring **culture** as *the ways in which groups of people do life together*.[5] Think about it this way: What makes your family different than your best friend's family? What makes your city or town different from the next city or town up the road? What makes Florida different from New Mexico? What makes Holland different from Sri Lanka? In each case, there are certain patterns of how the groups of people do life together. These patterns are influenced by everything from geography to climate to patterns of commerce.

The challenge with culture is that not all of these patterns are readily visible. One of the popular illustrations of culture is the comparison to an iceberg. The basic idea is that while certain elements of culture are readily visible at the top of the iceberg, such as clothing and food, the majority of culture is actually below the surface, making it more difficult to see, understand, and relate to.

So what makes up the bottom of the iceberg? At this level, you find values and beliefs that both undergird the visible behaviors and are shaped by them. For example, a culture that highly values competitiveness may demonstrate this through external behaviors like youth club sports.

BIG IDEA #1 REFLECTION

(Prepare)

1. Try to come up with a metaphor or analogy for culture by completing the following statement: Culture is (like) . . . .

2. How would you define culture?

---

4 Kroeber and Kluckhohn 1963 as cited in Condon and LaBrack, "Culture, Definition of."
5 The concept of culture is more complicated than simply "the ways in which groups of people do life together." For a more complete discussion, including culture as (semiotic) communication along with various metaphors and analogies for culture, see Condon and LaBrack (Ibid).However, for the purposes of the present handbook the definition given is sufficient.

(Sojourn)

3. Try to come up with a metaphor or analogy for culture by completing the following statement: Culture is (like) . . . .

4. Now that you have spent some time in another cultural context, how would you define culture?

5. If applicable, what do you notice about how your ideas of what culture is have changed?

(Return)

6. Try to come up with a metaphor or analogy for culture by completing the following statement: Culture is (like) . . . .

7. As you are returning to a cultural context where you used to live, how would you define culture?

8. What do you notice about how your ideas of what culture is have changed?

Big Idea #2:
Cultures are often (very) different from each other

If culture is how groups of people do life together, then people must be able to rely on their cultural patterns and norms to provide written and unwritten rules about how life works. Our cultures tell us how to greet people, what makes a good job candidate, how to interview, and how to express confidence and respect. We usually learn all of these things without ever having to read books on etiquette. Our cultures also tell us what success looks like, and they instill deep values about the relationship between people and task. What might be most important is that culture forms in us the crucial skill of recognizing and utilizing common sense.

The challenge is that cultural patterns are doing the same thing for someone from another part of town or another part of the planet. However, very often, this process happens differently for people from other cultural backgrounds. What my culture has decided looks like respect might look like arrogance in someone else's culture. Our cultures might define a successful job candidate in different, or even opposite, ways. Just imagine how different common sense could look. For example, my culture says that you look someone else in the eyes to show genuineness. Yet there are cultures in which eye contact is a sign of disrespect. If you and I have a conversation in which I keep looking into your eyes and you keep looking down, what a terribly confusing conversation we could have! You and I would both feel disrespected precisely because we were both trying to show respect to the other! And not only that, but my friends would know that I was doing it right because it's just *common sense* that looking in someone's eyes shows respect. Yet among your people group, your friends would know that you were doing it right because it's just *common sense* that looking down shows deference. Who's right?

BIG IDEA #2 REFLECTION

(Preparation)

1. What is one area of cultural difference you have noticed in the past?

2. How did it affect you?

(Sojourn)

3. What is one area of difference between your host culture and your home culture that you have noticed in the past week?

4. How did it affect you?

5. Since returning, what is an area of cultural difference you have noticed between the host culture you left behind and the home culture you have returned to?

6. How did it affect you?

Big Idea #3:
It's more complicated than we think it is

The following conversation between a teacher and his students exemplifies the use of cultural shortcuts in everyday life. The teacher starts by asking the students to describe this object:

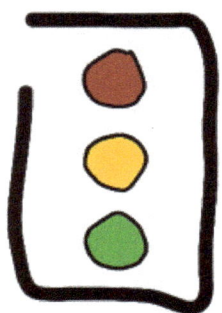

Teacher: What do you see?

Student: It's a stoplight!

Teacher: What do you see?

Student: A traffic signal!

Teacher: What do you see?

Student: A rectangular box with three circular lights—yellow, red, and green!

Teacher: What do you see?

Student: A drawing of a stoplight?

Teacher: Okay, now we're getting somewhere. What do you see in the drawing?

Student: Well, it looks like a rectangle, but it isn't quite, and your circles are drawn badly.

Teacher: Great, so you see a drawing of something kind of like a rectangle, with three badly drawn circles of different colors? Is that what everyone would see looking at this?

Student: Well, yeah, unless they were color blind.

Teacher: Okay, so would that change the color of the drawing?

Student: Well . . . kind of, but no, it doesn't. But it changes the way the person would see the drawing.

Teacher: Interesting. Tell me what the drawing means to you.

Student: Well, it's a stoplight for directing traffic.

Teacher: Okay, what do the different lights mean?

Student: Green means go, red means stop, and yellow means slow down.

Teacher: Are you sure that's what those mean? Let's take green, for example. What does it really mean?

Student: So you're saying it doesn't mean go? Hmm ... Well, I guess it means proceed through the intersection if conditions are safe.

Teacher: That seems like a good bet. I'm going to suggest that red doesn't really mean stop. What do you think it means?

Student: Maybe that we shouldn't go through the intersection. Unless we're already in the intersection when it turns red, in which case we should get out right away. Or unless we stop first and make a right-hand turn. Or, if we're at the intersection of two one- way streets, it might be possible to turn left, but you have to stop first.

Teacher: Okay, good. So what you're saying is that it's complicated?

Student: Yeah. And yellow means Speed Up!

Teacher: Or, more precisely, it means . . .

Student: I think it means make up your mind on how to be safe. Either get through the intersection or stop before you enter the intersection.

This little dialogue illustrates that we take a lot of things for granted. We constantly use shortcuts to make life around us easier to understand. We see a drawing and interpret it as a stoplight. Of course it isn't; it's a drawing. (And there is yet more complexity here—we are actually interpreting light reflecting off pigments; the pigments are actually absorbing all the colors except the one we see; not everyone's eyes and brains interpret colors the same way, etc.) We see a red light and say, "Oh, that means 'stop,'" but of course, in and of itself the red light doesn't mean anything at all. And yet we are largely able to function without talking about what red really means because, as a culture, we have stored that information as **tacit knowledge**. We don't have to think about it.

So let's recap what we know so far.

Big Idea #1: Culture is the way people do their stuff together.

Big Idea #2: Cultures are often (very) different from each other.

Big Idea #3: It's more complicated than we think it is.

These lead us to Big Idea #4.

(Sojourn)

1. What is one example of tacit knowledge from your home culture that you were unaware of before but have become aware of while on your sojourn?

Additional Notes

Big Idea #4:
Moving between cultures can be deeply disorienting

If we recognize that culture is the way people do their stuff together, that people do stuff in very different ways from each other, and that much of this is happening in our subconscious, it shouldn't be surprising that moving between cultures can be deeply disorienting.

Imagine that you have grown up in a culture where you start the day at around 7 o'clock. This shouldn't be too difficult for most American readers. You have your coffee, grab a bite to eat, and head to work. What time do you eat lunch? Around 12 o'clock is an approximate guess, and you probably wrap up your work-day around 5 or 6 o'clock. Pretty straightforward, right?

Now imagine that you find yourself in a culture where someone asks you to meet him at 6 o'clock for a meal on Tuesday. Tuesday comes, and you go through the workday looking forward to the evening meal. You show up at the restaurant at the appointed time, but your host doesn't show up. After a long and awkward period of drinking soda and waiting, you finally decide to head home, disappointed and hurt. The next day, your would-be host mentions that he was disappointed that you didn't join him yesterday, and could you reschedule for the following week?

What's happened? There are at least three possibilities. Really, there are hundreds, but we'll take three. Oftentimes in cross-cultural situations, the first possibility that comes to our minds is negative. Even if we don't normally assume the worst about people, we tend to misattribute behaviors we don't under-stand to bad character. In this case, for example, you might be likely to think that your host is not being totally straightforward in the relationship, or that he's at least not totally honest. After all, why can't he just admit that he forgot, instead of blaming you? Even though this seems like a very negative reaction, it is a surprisingly common one.

The second possibility is that you simply didn't wait long enough. In some cultures, times are simply ballpark estimates. Perhaps your host showed up at 8 o'clock, and he was surprised to find that you did not come. He might have been shocked to imagine that you were in fact there but had already left.

A third possibility is that you were late! In Ethiopia, for example, 6 o'clock falls closer to the middle of the day than to the end of it. What Americans would call 7 o'clock in the morning is called 1:00 daylight. Thus, noon, when the sun is at the highest point overhead, occurs around 6 o'clock rather than 12. So, if you might have been there at 7 o'clock, you were probably about six hours late!

The point of this section is not to consider different ways that time is understood in different cultures[6], but rather to demonstrate the real differences in perspective that are possible across cultures. These striking differences are found not just in relation to time but across all areas of what it means to be human. And in each case, most of the differences are primarily acknowledged in our tacit awareness, rather than overtly.

This means that when we cross cultures, we carry with us a guide map of how life works. In that map, we carry critical information like how to make friends; how to provide for our basic necessities like food, shelter, and going to the bathroom; and how to be successful. These basic things are normally quite natural for us in our home culture by the time we are engaging in cultural sojourns with Students International. We have successfully built our map of how the world works using the cultural patterns we have grown up with. This is also the case for **third-culture kids**[7] and **global nomads**,[8] although it plays out somewhat differently than for the general population. So, when we enter another culture and begin to figure out how to do life, we are already using a map of the world that is based in our own culture, but that we are usually not aware of.

The reason moving across cultures can be so deeply disorienting is that our map is often *wrong* in this new setting. Certain paths or roads look familiar, so we try to orient our map according to them, only to find out that they lead to places we weren't looking to go.

A friend of mine who came to the US for college told the humorous story of how he could not figure out how to exit the building where he lived. He explained that "your exits are not exits!" When leaving the dorm, he thought he was not supposed to take the elevator in case there was a fire (the sign read: "do not take elevator in case of fire"). So, he would take the stairs down to the bottom level. There are almost no basements in his home country, so he expected that the bottom level would lead him outside. First floor, to him, meant the first elevated floor, or what Americans call the second floor.

After finding himself still inside in the basement, he went to turn around and go back out the door, but there was a sign on it that said "fire door, keep closed." He grew increasingly concerned about the possibility of fire (signs like this are not common in his home country).[9] Then he saw

---

6 The differences in the way time is understood across cultures is a fascinating study! Several differences appear. One variation is in whether focus is placed on the past, present or future, as well as the extent to which these overlap (Trompenaars, *Riding the Waves of Culture*.). Another variation is in whether focus is placed on time or event (Mayers and Lingenfelter, *Ministering Cross-Culturally*.). Monochronic and polychronic understandings of time involve further variation, that affects perception of order, communication, and even conflict negotiation approaches (Ting-Toomey, *Communicating across Cultures*.).

7 Pollock and Van Reken, *Third Culture Kids*.

8 Schaetti, "Global Nomad, Third Culture Kid, Adult Third Culture Kid, Third Culture Adult: What Do They All Mean?"

9 The cultural value dimension of crisis/non-crisis orientation can help to explain this difference (Lingenfelter and Mayers, "God's Metaphor for Ministry: The Incarnation.")

a sign instructing readers to run clockwise on Mondays, Wednesdays, and Fridays and to run counterclockwise on Tuesdays, Thursdays, and Saturdays. Not realizing that he had stumbled onto the college's running track, he thought these signs were because of the risk of fire, so he started to run! He kept finding doors that said things he didn't understand (like "emergency exit, alarm will sound"), and it took hours before he found a way out of the building!

Even in less comic circumstances, the reality of mismatched maps is that they cause deep disturbances, as **sojourners** find themselves misinterpreted and unable to function or communicate effectively in their new cultural milieu.

BIG IDEA #4 REFLECTION
(Preparation)

1. Can you think of a time that you went somewhere new and felt disoriented by how people did things there? Examples include visiting an unfamiliar city with a different road layout, a grocery store that was laid out differently than what you expected, or spending time with a friend's family or your own extended family that may have had different patterns for familiar activities, or maybe a different way of thinking about politics, religion, or even sports!

2. How did those kinds of differences affect you? Do you remember any of the ways that you responded to them?

(Sojourn)

3. Since you have been away, what kinds of patterns have you noticed where people do things differently from what you would have expected?

4. Have you been disoriented – perhaps taken the wrong bus, walked down the wrong street, ordered the wrong food, or greeted someone incorrectly?

5. Have you encountered any major disorientation? Perhaps those provoked by differences in faith, politics, language, or role expectations?

6. How have those kinds of disorientations affected you?

(Return)

7. As you have returned, have you encountered moments of disorientation?

8. How have these affected you? Have they surprised you?

9. In what ways have those moments of disorientation been similar and different from the disorientation you experienced on your sojourn?

Using the wrong cultural map can be deeply disorienting – especially when certain
"landmarks" look familiar.

Big Idea #5:
The disorientation caused by crossing cultural barriers can be anticipated and reduced, but not eliminated

A student once told a colleague of mine that she wasn't going to experience **culture shock** because she had never been tired after flying before. Despite my friend's desperate attempts to explain the difference between **jet lag** and culture shock, she entered a six-month sojourn with the idea that once she caught up on her sleep, the worst would be behind her.

This underestimation of culture shock is not, by the way, limited to new sojourners. I had another student who had grown up as a third-culture kid who was certain that he would not experience culture shock because he had been back and forth between different cultures so many times. This individual had one of the worst experiences of culture shock I had seen up to that point, in part because a portion of his identity was based on the idea that he was so good at moving between cultures.

I have to shake my head when I hear seasoned business travelers explain that they never get culture shock. Why? Because everyone who enters deeply into another culture will experience culture shock (no matter how many times he or she has done it before).[10,11]

There is something about the human experience that causes us to be deeply affected when we encounter life that is understood in ways that are very different from what we are used to— even if we already know what to expect in the host culture. Through *planning, preparation,* and perhaps most importantly, *ongoing reflection,* sojourners can anticipate, reduce the effects of, and more effectively navigate culture shock. However, it cannot be entirely eliminated. In one of my favorite quotes from a very good book, Eva Hoffman[12] suggests:

> . . . *for all our sophisticated deftness of cross-cultural encounters, fundamental difference, when it's staring at you across the table from within the close-up face of a fellow human being, always contains an element of violation.*

The phenomenon of culture shock, even if it seems fatalistic, must be properly accounted

---

10 This is especially so if culture shock is understood not merely as a passive response process as indicated by Oberg ("Cultural Shock: Adjustment to New Cultural Environments.") but as an active process of navigating the affective, behavioral, and cognitive elements of cross-cultural contact (Ward, Bochner, and Furnham, *Psychology Culture Shock - Ed2.*). Thus, a person may be experiencing and enacting culture shock, including the identity negotiation and cognitive adaptation, regardless of whether s/he is aware of his/her doing so.

11 Culture shock is sometimes referred to as the 'occupational hazard of overseas living' (Kohls, *Survival Kit for Overseas Living.*).

12 Hoffman, *Lost in Translation.*

for. The only way to be in another culture and not experience culture shock is to fail to engage with the culture in a deep way, which is incompatible with the mission of Students International.

Moving forward

This chapter was designed to provide an overview to the realities involved with crossing cultures. The following chapters will deal in depth with ideas that will help you better navigate the sojourn, whether your own or that of a friend or family member.

Chapter Three addresses the process of transition, as applied to the cross-cultural sojourn.

Chapter Four looks more fully into the unique realities of culture shock and factors that increase the intensity of cross-cultural sojourns.

Chapter Five explores the preparation for and experience of a cross-cultural sojourn.

Chapter Six wraps up by looking at the unique challenges facing those who return from a cross-cultural sojourn, including advice for family and friends.

Chapter Seven is a consideration of common experiences of Christians who transition across cultures, especially when they are in a position to be recognized for their faith.

Students International's greatest successes are the result of cross-cultural and trans-national collaborations. The remainder of this handbook is designed to communicate the seriousness of cross-cultural transition and to better prepare you for your own success and for the success of those you lead.

BIG IDEA #5 AND CHAPTER TWO REFLECTION

(Preparation)

1. This chapter has provided a brief introduction to the idea of culture and how crossing from one cultural setting to another can be very disorienting. Are there any cultural differences that you expect will be challenging to you as you transition into life in your host site?

2. Today, how real does the idea of culture shock seem to you? Answering honestly, do you think it is likely that you will experience culture shock?

(Sojourn)

3. Does the idea of culture make more or less sense to you now than it did before you started your trip?

4. Do you think you have experienced culture shock on this trip? We will revisit this question in Chapter Four, so just answer with your initial response.

(Return)

5. In retrospect, do you think you experienced culture shock as part of your sojourn? If so, what was it like? Did you know that you were experiencing it as it happened?

6. As you return, do you think that the differences between your host culture and home culture will cause culture-shock-like disorientation? Why or why not?

Chapter Three:
The Process of Transition

Cross-cultural transition is not just a process of navigating culture – it is also a process of navigating transition itself. While there are several different ways to think about transitions, one of the most helpful models is from William Bridges.[13] Bridges suggests that we consider transitions as beginning with an ending, rather than with a beginning. On its face, this seems confusing, but it is actually a key to successfully navigating cultural transitions. The basic process of transition outlined by Bridges is as follows:

Ending → Transition Zone → Beginning

Thus, Bridges suggests that transitions begin with an ending and end with a beginning. Perhaps this is not so difficult to understand. For example, as a caterpillar transforms into a butterfly, it must first end being a caterpillar. It then goes through the chrysalis stage of transition, and it ends the transition with a new beginning as a butterfly. Whether our own transitions will result in anything as lovely as a butterfly is irrelevant to the question of how transitions occur.[14]

Big Idea #6:
Begin with the endings

Before people embark on a transition, whether into a new culture or into the process of returning home, I challenge them to develop a list of at least five things that are ending in their lives as a result of the upcoming transition (there is space to do this on one of the following pages).

---

13 Bridges, *Transitions*.

14 The Apostle Paul seems to indicate something similar – that as new life begins in Christ that the old self passes away (Romans 6:6; Galatians 2:20). Thus, the beginning of the Christian life is also the ending of the "former way of life" (Ephesians 4:22). The comparison between cultural transition and the initiation of the Christian life is certainly imperfect, but it is helpful to see that the new beginning contains a powerful ending. Yet, as Paul also indicates in his letters to the Colossians (3:5) and the Ephesians (4:22) although there is a clear ending of the old self, there remains much transition as Christians seek to stop living according to the old patterns and to live according to the Spirit.

I have found this process to be useful for college students and career missionaries alike – it is often surprising how many endings we unintentionally overlook.[15]

As many people are more used to thinking in terms of adding to their lives than to taking things away, this exercise can be challenging for them. Consider this, though: a student who travels to Guatemala for the first time might be experiencing the following endings:

- She will no longer be a person who hasn't been to Guatemala (or perhaps Latin America if this is her first time to the region).

- She will no longer be a "normal" college student who spends all of her semesters on campus.

- Her status in her friend group will change.

- She will have to give up the job she has been working at part-time, with no guarantee of getting it back.

- Some of her ignorance and naiveté will be lost.

On the face of it, these might seem like small or expected changes for someone who has decided to travel internationally. However, these can actually be very traumatic. Perhaps the most traumatic component is the last one—the loss of ignorance. It can be very troubling to befriend people whose lives are very different from your own, because there are certain things that you simply cannot un-know, such as the suffering of others. For other young people, sojourns such as this mark in very profound ways the end of their childhood.

This process of discovering **endings** is relevant for any kind of cross-cultural sojourn. For businesspeople who are relocating for work, there is another set of endings that might be difficult to recognize before they happen:

- Their role in local organizations will end. Whether church, clubs, politics, or sports associations, it is simply impossible to maintain your local affiliations in the same way when not present.

- Their influence in the office will diminish. Even though overseas assignments can be a significant step up, they rarely bring more direct influence in the day-to-day operations

---

15 The process of identifying endings is quite different from Covey's principle that highly effective people "begin with the end in mind." Whereas Covey's idea involves the creative imagining of what can be, I advocate an honest reckoning of what will no longer be. (https://www.stephencovey.com/7habits/7habits-habit2.php)

of the office.

- Certain friendships will likely end. This is often difficult for people to believe in an age of instant global communication. My students have been shocked to find that even being gone for just four months can be enough to end friendships that they thought were strong before they left.

- Their sense of what is possible will change. Even the introduction of new possibilities is its own kind of ending, as people find out that their former view was too limited, thus ending it.

- Their advancement in your organization will become less straightforward. International assignments complicate advancement within most organizations, largely because most organizations are unable to adequately help their staff reintegrate upon return. The process of reintegration will be discussed in greater detail in Chapter Five.

Of course there are a host of other changes that depend on the length of a sojourn. It is worth noting that endings can result even from very short trips abroad. By way of example, it is possible that even a two-week trip abroad could lead to the end of feeling understood by friends and family. Similarly, such trips often lead to the end of certain myopic perspectives. While this can arguably be a good thing, the truth is that these endings carry a cost.

Lest you think that these endings apply only to college students and businesspeople, let's consider the ways in which they apply to missionaries. A group of missionaries I once trained identified each of the following endings in their own lives as a result of their time abroad:

- The end of:
  - "Normal" patterns of life, such as going to the grocery store, post office, walks around the neighborhood, etc.
  - Patterns of interaction and ability to maintain both important and casual relationships
  - Certain parts of identity, such as being from a particular town, being recognized, having your affiliations (school, sports team, clubs) be meaningful
  - The planning stage of preparation for the time abroad
  - Questions about the next steps (these were replaced with new questions, but the old questions were no longer relevant)
  - Attendance at a particular church
  - The end of a mentoring relationship (as a mentor or a mentee)

- Being known by neighbors, coworkers, barista's, etc.

- Being competent in the culture in which they were living

- Faith in their own organization to adequately lead and take care of them

- A romanticized view of mission(s)

- Expectations for support on the field from supervisors, field leaders, and people back home

Clearly some of these endings could be more troublesome than others. The key is to recognize that such endings really do occur and to try and identify them so that they can be adequately processed.

> **On refugees:** It is important to note that I have been describing the circumstances of willful (volitional) sojourners. However, there are many people in the world who find themselves in transition who would not have chosen to relocate if their circumstances had not forced them to do so. It is especially important that refugees (economic, political, disaster, etc.) come to terms with the endings in their lives. It is also imperative that those who serve refugees recognize the endings and losses that refugees have experienced and will continue to experience. Many of these endings do not become apparent immediately, surfacing in waves as life unfolds in their new "home." It is especially important to give space for refugees to mourn these endings, as many of them are absolutely permanent.

BIG IDEA #6 REFLECTION
(Preparation)

1. Identify and describe at least five endings you expect to experience as you prepare for your sojourn:

   1)

   2)

   3)

   4)

   5)

2. How do you think experiencing these endings might affect you?

(Sojourn)

3. Identify and describe at least five endings you actually experienced as a result of beginning your sojourn:

1)

2)

3)

4)

5)

4. How do you think experiencing these endings affected you?

5. Did any of these endings surprise you?

(Return)

6. Reflect on the endings that happened when you began your sojourn. If you haven't already recorded them above, go ahead and do so. Then, identify and describe at least five endings you are experiencing now as return from your sojourn:

1)

2)

3)

4)

5)

7. Consider adding the following endings, if applicable: a feeling of belonging in the host culture, feeling at home in the host culture, a sense of understanding of your own culture, the end of certain friendships or relationships (or the ending of a stage within a relationship).

8. How do you think experiencing these endings (from questions 6 and 7) might affect you?

Big Idea #7:
Engage the transition zone

In developing his model for transitions, Bridges suggested that the middle stage could be called the **transition zone** or the **neutral zone**. For some, the idea that this stage could be called neutral is very troubling, because it is often a very difficult stage. I find it helpful to think of it as similar to putting a car into neutral. It doesn't matter how much you push on the gas, the car simply doesn't have the ability to propel itself while in neutral. This is analogous to the experience of being in the midst of a cross-cultural transition.

The sojourner is thrust into the neutral zone by the series of endings just discussed, and these endings often introduce a high level of ambiguity. The sojourner may be stuck thinking, "Well, I'm no longer the way I was, but nothing has replaced that yet." For example, the successful businesswoman who was active in her community may be surprised to find that she is no longer receiving regular praise from those around her. Thus, her status as a force for good in the community is no longer affirmed, causing it, in a sense, to end. Yet, at this point, her former status as a force for good has not been replaced by anything. In this in-between state, she is no longer, and also not yet, affirmed as a force for good in the community.

CROSS-CULTURAL TRANSITION HANDBOOK ✠

The void caused by this in-between space is unsettling for most people; it is also experienced multiple times in the course of ordinary life (for example, at high school graduation or beginning a new degree, getting married or divorced, gaining or losing a job, at the birth of a child or the death of a loved one). Yet in the cross-cultural setting, this naturally occurring transitional phenomena is exacerbated by the mismatched cultural maps described in Chapter Two. For example, the businesswoman mentioned above might find herself unable to replace meaningful community-based friendships quickly due to mismatched cultural patterns surrounding the interplay between work and pleasure. Even more frustrating (especially but not only for women) can be mismatched expectations around gender roles, which might lead people to feel unfamiliar and unwelcome restrictions. Further differences around cultural ideas and patterns related to time, space, motivation, communication, and nature, and it's easy to see that navigating the transition zone can be a whole lot more complicated when in another culture![16]

The temptation many sojourners face is to rush through the transition zone. This is particularly so for sojourners with a high value on task and efficiency, which is the case for many Students International participants. The discomfort brought on by so much not-knowing and in-between-ness can be motivation enough to encourage even very introspective people to try and push past this stage into the new beginnings. Bridges explains that our approach to transition is often like that of crossing a street—only a fool, we reason, would hang out in the middle where it is most dangerous and uncomfortable. Yet transitioning across cultures is not the same as crossing a street.

What I have observed is that those who press *into* the difficulties of the neutral zone are often rewarded in two ways. First, they gain tremendous insights into themselves and their own culture that can inspire them for years (or even decades) to come. Second, having adequately processed this movement from a kind of death into a kind of rebirth, they encounter far fewer unresolved tensions that unexpectedly flare up well after the transition has been "completed." They are, on the whole, more peaceful.

On the other hand, people who press *past* the transition zone as though it were just a passing cold are robbed of some very important insights into themselves and their culture. Yet more damaging is the cost of pressing through: certain wounds inflicted by the process (and intentionally or unintentionally by other people) are allowed to fester—sometimes for years. This is a most unsatisfactory outcome.

I have unfortunately observed this pattern in American missionaries and their families, who often return to the US about once every four years for furlough or home assignment. This time,

---

16 This discomfort is not necessarily alleviated by returning home due to the cross-cultural nature of the return. This idea is developed in Chapter Six.

far from being one of respite, is often busier than life in their adoptive country. Through keeping a nearly nonstop schedule of traveling, speaking, conferences, and meetings, missionaries and their families are able to be physically present in the US for a year without ever really processing the transition. This is part of why the third culture kid mentioned in Chapter Two had so much trouble with culture shock. Even though he had been back and forth between different countries for years, he had never been taught how to process the cultural transition.

You might be wondering at this point just how you will be able to successfully navigate the transition zone. Here is a short list of suggested practices:

- Make sure you begin with the endings—identifying these, and mourning them properly, is key to a successful transition.

- Engage in regular reflection, ideally with guided questions that have been tailored to your situation.

- **Journaling** is tremendously positive for successful navigation of cultural differences. Recording events may prove helpful, but one of the most important uses for a journal is the honest assessment of your emotions during the day. Added bonus: Later readings of the journals will often reveal important cultural data that you can't see at the time.

- Don't check out! It is often tempting to check out through media like books and movies, or through communication tools like Skype, social media, cell phones, and the internet; this is ultimately self-limiting and can short-circuit the useful process of the neutral zone. Hiding out in the **expat** community is another mode of checking out that should be avoided. Although some connections with fellow expats can be helpful, they can also become ways to hide from the cultural transition.

- Do plan for ways that you can cope with the stresses, and allow yourself some (but not too much) downtime.

- More suggestions for effective coping are presented in Chapter Five.

BIG IDEA #7 REFLECTION

(Preparation)

1. Can you think of a transition in the past (cross-cultural or not) where you have experienced the neutral zone? What was it like? What worked well for navigating it and what didn't?

2. Which of the suggested practices for transitioning the neutral zone appeals most to you? Why?

(Sojourn)

3. Have you experienced or been experiencing the neutral zone as a result of your transition to the host culture? Describe your experience of the neutral zone up to this point.

4. Did you at any time feel any of the following?
    1) This isn't what I signed up for

2) I want to go home

3) I'm not sure who I am

4) What am I doing here?

5) Why does God feel so distant?

5. If so, how have you navigated those feelings?

6. Up to this point which of the following has been your primary strategy for dealing with the neutral zone (if applicable)?

1) Push past it (keep busy)

2) Ignore it

3) Internalize it (the problem is with me)

4) Externalize it (the problem is with someone else, the host culture, or the organization)

7. What coping mechanisms have you used as you have moved through the neutral zone?

8. Sometimes people make decisions they end up regretting while navigating the neutral zone – Are there decisions that you have made that you will need to revisit as you look to move forward?

9. What support did you have as you moved through the neutral zone?

10. Despite the discomfort of the neutral zone, there are often also really good things that happen during that time. What are some good things from the transition time that you want to remember later on?

11. What might Christ have been revealing to you about himself through this transition time?

12. Earlier you described at least five endings related to your transition. What have you done to mourn the passing of each of them?

   1)

   2)

   3)

   4)

   5)

13. Journaling is one of the suggestions for successfully navigating the transition zone. What positive coping mechanisms like this might you be able to use to better your chances of success in the neutral zone?

14. It is not uncommon for Christians to experience a sense of distance between themselves and God during the transition zone. There are all sorts of reasons for this, many of which are not the "fault" of the sojourner. How do you feel your relationship is with God during this time?

15. Do you have any thoughts about steps you feel led to take to draw nearer to him?

(Return)

16. As you return home, it is likely that you will experience the neutral zone again. Reflecting on your previous experience(s) with the neutral zone, what can you do to avoid skipping past it while also coping in healthy ways?

Additional Notes

Big Idea #8:
Allow the new beginnings to breathe

As the transition process winds down, it is helpful to identify **new beginnings**. It is important not to do this too soon, because people sometimes think that they are closer to the end of the transition than they actually are – this is somewhat like a mirage that is present within the neutral zone, and mirages do not make for solid new beginnings. After a while, though, you will notice the ambiguity beginning to diminish, and new insights will begin to present themselves. In general, based on experience (though not on hard research), I expect the first two stages of transition to last a combined minimum of three months (sometimes even more than a year!) before sojourners can begin to really see the new beginnings.

Although it is tempting to rush into new beginnings, premature commitments can cause lasting pain or broken promises. It can be helpful to be a little bit tentative at this stage. At the same time, this is a wonderful time for exploration of new possibilities. Perhaps the new cultural setting will allow new elements of yourself to come out that you never expected, such as discovering the love of art or cooking, finding a new means of linguistic expression, or finding the seed thoughts for a new business concept.

As these new realities begin to crystallize, you will realize that you are, in some ways, a different version of yourself. This can actually be very frightening to some people, and it is therefore really important to keep track of these new changes. Again, I recommend a journal.

BIG IDEA #8 REFLECTION

(Preparation)

1. As you prepare to go, what do you hope changes about you while you are gone?

2. As you prepare to go, what do you hope does not change about you while you are gone?

(Sojourn)

3.   What new patterns have you established while on your sojourn?

4.   What is different about you now that you hope stays different?

5.   What is different about you that you aren't sure about or don't like?

(Return)

6.   As you return home, what new beginnings are important for you to keep?

7.   What new beginnings that emerged while you were gone may be surprising for people back home?

Big Idea #9:
Pick up the thread of continuity

Amidst all of the change experienced in the previous three steps, it might seem like the process of cross-cultural transition involves a complete redefinition of the self. This, fortunately, is not a necessary outcome of cross-cultural transition. One of Bridges' most important ideas is that of the **thread of continuity**.

Sometime toward the end of the neutral zone (during which it can seem like your whole sense of self is threatened), it becomes easier to see that in spite of all the changes, there is actually a lot that has stayed the same. Not only that, but this is the stage in which it is possible to identify the most important parts of what you intend to accomplish or who you intend to be in life. Picking up the thread of continuity is essentially the process of stating to yourself what it was that was true about you before, has been true about you in the transition (even if you forgot), and will be true about you moving forward.

For example, as I moved through the process of transition after losing a job, there came a point when certain themes reemerged, and I saw that in some ways I would be even better able to pursue what I had always cared about. In fact, I realized that the job had actually been preventing me from pursuing some things that were really important to me. Mind you, this insight did not come right away. Still, it is an important step to recognize that at some point in the transition process, you will have the opportunity to pick up the thread of continuity, moving forward with a recognition of who you always have been and who you will be.

For the Christ-follower, if it has been the case that God has felt distant during the transition, it is sometimes in the picking up the thread of continuity that your sense of walking with God will return. This is encouraging in part because during the neutral zone some people will encounter deep doubts about their identity in Christ. Very often the resolution of the neutral zone is accompanied by a reaffirmation of one's identity in Christ, wherein "the Spirit Himself testifies with our spirit that we are God's children" (Romans 8:16).

Elements of Transition Process Over Time

Identify Endings	Transition Zone / Neutral Zone	Discover Beginnings
_____		_____
_____		_____
_____		_____
_____		_____
_____		_____

Pick up the Thread of Continuity as the
Transition Zone Ends

While this chapter has dealt with the process of cross-cultural transition, we have only touched on the idea of culture shock. The next chapter will introduce you to culture shock and the various factors that make crossing cultures more intense.

BIG IDEA #9 REFLECTION

(Preparation)

1. Can you recall a time in the past that you went through a transition (of any kind) and then, coming out the other side of it, rediscovered things about yourself that had been true before?

(Sojourn)

2. Since beginning your sojourn have you at any point thought any of the following?

    1) "Oh, that's right. I remember that about me"?

    2) "Hey, maybe I can do this"?

3) "Now I know why I'm here"?

3. What new have you discovered about yourself as a result of the transition you have been experiencing?

4. What remains unchanged about you, despite the transition you have been experiencing?

5. What new have you discovered about Christ since beginning your sojourn?

6. What remains unchanged about who Jesus is regardless of your sojourn? And, do these things seem true to you today?

(Return)

7. As you return, you will very likely go through the transition process all over again. What do you hope remains true about you by the time you come out the other side of the neutral zone and pick up the thread of continuity?

8. Since returning, have you at any point thought any of the following?
    1) "Oh, that's right. I remember that about me"?

    2) "Hey, maybe I can do this"?

    3) "Now I know why I'm here"?

9. What new did have you discovered about yourself as a result of the transition back home that you have been experiencing?

10. What remains unchanged about you, despite the transition back home that you have been experiencing?

11. What new have you discovered about Christ since returning to your 'home' country?

12. What remains unchanged about who Jesus is regardless of your return home? And, do these things seem true to you today?

Chapter Four:
Culture Shock

Culture shock is an idea that is familiar to many people,[17] but I have been surprised by how few actually have some sense of what culture shock is and how to deal with it effectively. This chapter presents a brief overview of the topic.

Big Idea #10:
Culture shock is caused by cumulative disorientation

Culture shock can be understood as a response to the **cumulative disorientation** caused by exposure to (and especially immersion in) another culture. This means, for example, that someone who has been in another culture for just one week would not be experiencing culture shock, as it is difficult to experience accumulated effects of disorientation in that amount of time. It is possible that such a visitor would be experiencing culture *stress*, but culture *shock* results from deep and sustained contact with another culture.

Similarly, the way we are using the idea, it is not possible that any single event, or what Storti calls a cultural incident, can cause culture shock. For example, if you were to have a particularly difficult conversation with a member of the host culture, it would not be useful to label that experience as "culture shock." You might be able to call it a cultural clash or cultural miscommunication, but in and of itself the conversation would not be a culture shock.

One of the reasons that it is important to understand culture shock as a cumulative experience, is that the isolated events that stand out as being relevant to culture shock will often be confusing on their own. For example, I have had students say that they actually like the dirt outside all around them when first visiting a particular developing nation—there is, they have said, something uniquely good about the quality of this red dirt.

---

17 Originally conceptualized by Oberg ("Cultural Shock: Adjustment to New Cultural Environments.") and popularized by authors like Kohls (*Survival Kit for Overseas Living.*) and Storti (*The Art of Crossing Cultures.*). Kohls and Storti are particularly useful for readers looking to go beyond the basic introduction presented in this handbook. A more academic source, for readers wanting to go yet further is Ward, Bochner, and Furnham, *Psychology Culture Shock - Ed2*.

Yet within a month of their arrival, these same students have come to loathe the ubiquity of the dirt. It is everywhere—not just on the streets, but in their clothes and beds, on their mangoes, and in their books and computers. In this case, it might be tempting to suggest that the second experience (the bad dirt) is culture shock, whereas the first (the good dirt) is not. In fact—and this is important—*both* of these sentiments are expressions of culture shock because both are reactions to sustained contact with unfamiliar stimuli.

In the face of disorientation caused by stimuli such as language, climate, and cultural patterns ranging from hygiene to cuisine to traffic to business and on and on, many people go through a somewhat patterned (and therefore often predictable) set of steps, discussed in the next section.

BIG IDEA #10 REFLECTION

(Preparation)

1. Which of these examples might be categorized as culture shock, and which as cultural stressors or cultural incidents? Why?

   1) Being served squid cooked in its own ink for the first time for your first meal in a restaurant in your new location.

   2) Growing frustration at your apparent inability to find food you know how to cook at the grocery store, despite weeks of trying.

   3) Hearing the imam's calls to prayer after being in a new country for three months.

   4) Bungee jumping with your fellow students.

   5) After being in a new location for four months, taking an afternoon siesta because all the stores are closed.

   6) Feeling inexplicably exhausted after a couple of months of living in another country.

2. As the reader may have noticed, not all of the above qualify as culture shock. (1) is better understood as a cultural incident, which would be stressful for some and not for others. (3) and (5) will be stressful to some and not to others. It may contribute to culture shock but is not "a culture shock." (4), if not a normal type of activity for a person, could be done as a result of culture shock, but is not itself culture shock. (2) and (6) are perhaps the best examples of culture shock – why?

(Sojourn)

3. Identify at least 5 cultural stressors that you have experienced since arriving in your host country.

    1)

    2)

    3)

    4)

    5)

4. Recount a culturally stressful incident that has happened since arriving in your host country.

5. What sources of disorientation have you experienced since being here? How have they affected you?

(Return)

6. As you return, what kinds cultural stressors do you expect to experience? Or, what cultural stressors have you experienced since returning?

7. Describe a culturally stressful incident that you have experienced since returning.

8. Have you begun to experience an accumulated sense of disorientation since returning? What has that been like? Did you expect it or did it take you by surprise?

Big Idea # 11:
Culture shock follows a relatively predictable pattern

Although culture shock can be a tremendously challenging experience, it does at least tend to follow a predictable pattern. Familiarity with this pattern makes it easier to navigate successfully. While not everybody experiences the stages in the same way, and not everybody experiences all of them, the general order is emotional high; disenchantment, discouragement, and depression; and confidence and competence.

emotional high

In many cases, the first stage of culture shock is an **emotional high**. This is not true for everyone, but many people—especially people who have chosen to have the cross-cultural experience—initially experience being in the new culture as a good thing. It is not uncommon, in the first few weeks of a sojourn, for most stimuli to be interpreted through this frame. This is what caused my students to think that the dirt was so wonderful.

Importantly, many tourists never leave this so-called **honeymoon stage**, leading many Americans who have traveled to think that cultural differences are rather insignificant but very pleasant facts of life. Food, dress, and music are particularly apparent during this stage and are experienced as wonderful. This is the experience of culture that a person might encounter visiting Disney's Epcot center —safe, fascinating, and fun.

disenchantment, discouragement, and depression

The first stage, is bound to come to an end because this emotionally high experience of difference apparently cannot be sustained for longer than one or two months. For example, eventually even the most optimistic and sociable American may be overcome by the thought that while it is nice to spend a couple of hours a day socializing over tea, as happens in some West African cultures, it would really be nice to get more things done during that time.

Eventually, such differences in patterns and values[18] become frustrating to the point of being overwhelming. This is often accompanied by the realization that host-culture people *actually* live life this way! That realization is accompanied by the twin awareness that if they live life like this, they must not live the way we do. It is almost as though we thought that the hosts were kind of kidding, and that deep down we really all have the same need to be efficient that Americans do. By the way, this also works the other way. Short-term visitors to America are often very appreciative of our efficiency, innovation, and egalitarian access to the markets. Yet after several months here, they may begin to long for the hierarchies, stability, and structure that we eschew in favor of being able to move quickly. Depending on a person's level of intercultural competence[19] the differences may or may not be interpreted as cultural – they may be simply seen as personality issues, for example. However, the repeated attempts to use one's own cultural map (recall Chapter Two) and the failure of that map to adequately explain the world in the host culture context, leads to the end of the honeymoon period.

This second stage, which begins with **disenchantment**, almost always deteriorates further. Initially, this might look like a kind of growing **apathy** or **ambivalence** regarding the host culture. However, this feeling will often sink into a passionate dislike (or even hatred) for the host culture. There are several factors at work here that cause this emotionally heightened response.

1. The sojourner experiences normal **homesickness** that accompanies being away from one's own place and people for an extended period of time (apparent even within very similar cultures—for example, a Californian visiting relatives in Washington will often experience homesickness after a couple of months).

2. The demands of the sojourn normally increase after the first couple of months. There is often a real or imagined grace period at the beginning of the sojourn to allow for a transition. However, after a couple of months, it is expected that you will be able to function at high capacity. Neither hosts nor sponsors back home (like bosses or teachers) are

---

18 Cultural values orientations represent a way to study patterned differences between cultures. Such differences are demonstrated by behavior but are rooted in deeply held beliefs and values, which are often unknown (tacit) even to the people that hold them. The concept was originated by Kluckhohn and Strodtbeck (*Variations in Value Orientations.*) and developed by Condon and Yousef (*An Introduction to Intercultural Communication.*). Authors who have contributed to this study from missions perspective include Hesselgrave (*Communicating Christ Cross-Culturally, Second Edition.*), Hiebert (*Anthropological Insights for Missionaries.*), and Lingenfelter and Mayers (*Ministering Cross-Culturally.*) More about cultural value orientations can be found in my book *Being Intercultural.*

19 Bennett, "A Developmental Approach to Training for Intercultural Sensitivity"; Bennett, *Basic Concepts of Intercultural Communication,* 1998; Bennett, *Basic Concepts of Intercultural Communication,* 2013.

generally expecting you to have difficulty after the initial adjustment—especially if you sent back rosy reports during the emotionally high stage.

3. By this point in the sojourn, many of the deeper cultural differences have begun to be really apparent. However, there has not been enough time to develop and hone skills to be effective in the host culture. Thus, the distance between what you need to be learning and your actual level of functionality becomes apparent, which can be especially discouraging. Moreover, by this point, sojourners have usually started to uncover some realities about the host culture that they find troubling but have not yet been able to process.

This stage is not a straightforward downward slope, as there will often be small and moderate successes along the way. However, sometimes these successes give rise to even greater disappointment. This is especially true for language learning. Increasing your ability to conjugate verbs, for example, may result in realizing that there is a whole tense that you have not been using or have developed patterns of misusing.

I have included the word *depression* in the title of this subsection, and it is important to clarify what I mean here. Recalling that culture shock is cumulative, the combined effects of continued disappointment, sadness (as in missing home), and frustration can lead to emotional, mental, and physical fatigue. In concert, these symptoms can present in a way that is very similar to clinical depression. There are two important things to know about this. First, if a person is on medication for depression, this is almost always a bad time to stop taking your meds. Sometimes people view a cross-cultural transition as a time to reinvent themselves, but never stop taking your antidepressants while on a sojourn without thoroughly consulting with a mental health or medical professional.

Second, although culture shock often looks like depression, most people are able to exit it without the assistance of (new) medications or counseling. Although culture shock is cumulative, it is also transitory, meaning that it almost always passes with time. If the depressive symptoms of culture shock are hanging around without any noticeable improvement, it is wise to seek professional psychological assistance, especially as culture shock may be related to adjustment disorder.[20]

An alternative reaction can happen within the disenchantment stage, which should be briefly mentioned. Sometimes people who are experiencing culture shock will, for any number of reasons, not feel that their frustration is with the host culture. Instead, they may experience similar revulsion for their own culture and/or their team. Some will also refrain from blaming the differences that they experience on the host culture and instead assume that the problems are either with themselves or the host organization. While every organization has its problems, students who are unusually critical of Students International may be directing their culture-shock induced angst at the organization without realizing it. The next big idea will more fully address the normal symptoms of culture shock, as it can be difficult to recognize. For now, we will turn to the more encouraging news about culture shock—the way out!

confidence and competence

After a period of what can feel like a free fall toward personal and professional **disintegration**, sojourners will usually realize that they have begun to stabilize. A new normal gradually arises, with patterns of living that become more predictable and productive. This is not something

---

20 Lucas, "Over-Stressed, Overwhelmed, and Over Here: Resident Directors and the Challenges of Student Mental Health Abroad."
21 Kohls, *Survival Kit for Overseas Living.*

that you can force to happen on your own timeline, but for nearly everyone who goes through culture shock, there is a moment when you realize that things are not as bad as they were before. Slowly but surely, you begin to develop specific competencies related to your responsibilities. At the same time, you begin to develop social skills that are appropriate for the context. Finally, you also begin to develop realistic expectations about communication with friends, families, and institutions and organizations back home.

This period is a relatively long process of trial and error, and it usually involves one or two major setbacks. However, the general trajectory is back toward emotional stability and efficacy. As you grow into the new culture, you may begin the real process of adapting to the culture. This is to some degree dependent on your level of **intercultural competence**. Regardless of your level of intercultural competence, this is a stage of increasing confidence and usually signals the slow, but real, end of culture shock—unless and until you return home. Chapter Five deals with the process of returning home and the struggles that often accompany this transition.

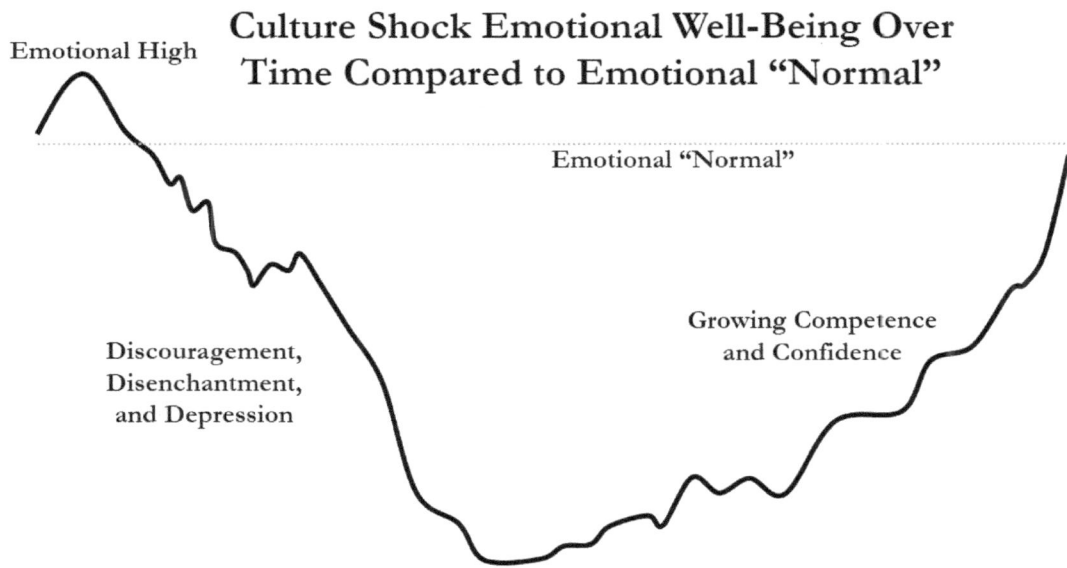

Culture Shock Emotional Well-Being Over Time Compared to Emotional "Normal"

Emotional High

Emotional "Normal"

Discouragement,
Disenchantment,
and Depression

Growing Competence
and Confidence

BIG IDEA #11 REFLECTION

(Preparation)

1. As people experience culture shock they can acknowledge or disregard it. If you have experienced culture shock in the past, how did you navigate the process? If you have not experienced culture shock in person, describe your observations of another who has.

2. Right now, do you expect that you will experience culture shock on your sojourn?

(Sojourn)

3. Did you experience an emotional high when your sojourn started? Describe what the beginning of your sojourn was like.

4. Have you experienced the stage of disenchantment and discouragement? If so, was your angst primarily directed at the host culture, your own culture, your team, Students International, or somewhere else?

5. Have you begun to develop confidence and competence and to return to a more familiar emotional status? What has that journey been like for you?

6. Overall, do you feel like the graphic above represents your journey through culture shock up to this point? If so, where do you think you might be today relative to the line on the graphic? If not, draw your own and explain it.

7. What has surprised you about your own culture shock journey up to this point?

8. If you have experienced culture shock during this sojourn, how did you navigate the process? If you don't feel like you experienced culture shock in person, describe your observations of another who has.

(Return)

9. As you return home, do you expect that you will experience culture shock again? Why or why not?

10. Since you have been home, which of the stages have you experienced so far?

11. If you have experienced angst have you directed it more toward your own culture or the host culture you have left behind? Or have you directed it more toward your friends, family, school, organization, or yourself?

12. Does the graphic above represent your journey since returning? If the graphic does represent your journey, identify where you might be right now and place a mark on the line. If not, draw your own transition curve here:

13. What has surprised you about your own culture shock journey up to this point?

14. Culture shock and its patterns can be acknowledged or disregarded. If you experienced culture shock during your return home, how did you navigate the process? If you don't feel like you experienced culture shock in person, describe your observations of another who did.

Big Idea #12:
Train yourself to recognize the symptoms of culture shock

I am often surprised at how people who are right in the midst of culture shock fail to recognize it in themselves. They often assume that their malaise is due to something else, and they are at times even hostile to the idea that they are experiencing culture shock. I think that sometimes people view it as a kind of failure, which it is not. In fact, I tend more to think it is evidence that you are actually engaging with the experience, and it is therefore often a good (albeit very uncomfortable) sign.

I am including a list of symptoms that my students have found very helpful. I recommend reading through this list at least once every couple of weeks while in the midst of a cross-cultural transition, to see whether you are experiencing culture shock. These ideas have been adapted from L. Robert Kohls' very useful book.[21] (I recommend picking up a copy.)

- ongoing anxiety or boredom – especially if these are not normal experiences for you

- feelings of homesickness, missing home an unusual amount (includes missing the host country when returning home)

- a feeling of being helpless or unable to take care of yourself even if you are trying hard to do so, or an inability to try hard to take care of yourself, or the feeling that no one will let you take care of yourself

- ongoing feelings of depression, sadness, or inadequacy

- fatigue that doesn't resolve even with an appropriate amount of sleep (after jet lag has resolved, if applicable)

- an exaggerated or new inability to make decisions

- increased, new, or overwhelming self-doubt

- unexplained emotions and emotional outbursts like anger, weeping, or laughter

- an irrational belief that others are intentionally sabotaging you

- physical (psychosomatic) illnesses, persistent colds, difficulties with digestion beyond normal difficulties with food, altitude, or other such adjustment (this can be difficult to determine)

- physically hiding away from others, such as by spending excessive amounts of time in your bedroom, hotel room, apartment, or dorm room

- being physically present but mentally withdrawing, such as by daydreaming

- spending large amounts of time reading or watching TV or movies, or on social media

- spending large amounts of time sleeping

- interacting only with people who are culturally like you (or, in some cases, only with people who are culturally different from you)

- having an inability to pay attention to others or to tasks for a long period of time

---

21 Kohls, *Survival Kit for Overseas Living*.

- losing the ability to study or work effectively, or to think clearly

- eating excessively or compulsively (comfort eating)

- drinking mood-altering drinks like coffee or alcohol excessively or compulsively

- a new or exaggerated need for cleanliness, or an unusually heightened awareness of un-cleanliness

- irritability and irrational anger

- noticeably increased tension with coworkers, teammates, peers, or family

- the exaggeration of controlling tendencies—even if these are for the "benefit" of others

- an increased reliance on simplified frames for understanding differences—such as using stereotypes to understand your own or the host culture. This can also be applied to gender, race, class or other such differences.

- smoldering or expressive hostility toward members of the host culture or of your own culture

- unusual levels of verbal, physical, or sexual aggressiveness. Physical aggressiveness can include road rage as well as other kinds of hostility.

It may surprise you to learn that nearly all of my students have experienced at least two-thirds of these symptoms at some point during their cross-cultural transition. It is important to understand that these are symptoms of culture shock for two reasons. First, imagine that you have recently arrived in another country and find yourself exhibiting these symptoms but don't realize that they are being caused by culture shock. I have seen people in this state—they begin to assume that the symptoms are actually problems with themselves. ("I don't even recognize myself! I'm not this mean of a person!") For this reason, understanding these symptoms helps people to have more grace for themselves and their companions through the culture shock process. Second, recognizing culture shock at work in yourself can alert you to the reality that you may be attempting to cope with the stress in a way that is ultimately unhealthy. This idea is addressed more fully in Big Idea #17.

BIG IDEA #12 REFLECTION

(Preparation)

1. There are many potential symptoms of culture shock. What can you do to regularly evaluate whether or not you are experiencing these indicators and whether they are related to your own experience of culture shock?

(Sojourn)

2. Have you experienced any of these symptoms on your present trip? Which ones?

3. If so, did you recognize them as being related to culture shock? Explain.

4. Have you observed these symptoms in anyone else on this sojourn? Do you think that person might be experiencing culture shock?

(Return)

5. Have you experienced any of these symptoms on your present trip? Which ones?

6. If so, did you recognize them as being related to culture shock? Explain.

7. What plan do you have to watch for the symptoms of culture shock in your return home? If you find that you are experiencing culture shock, how will you address it?

Note: This book is intended as a general guide and will not be appropriate for all situations. I especially recommend *The Psychology of Culture Shock* (second edition) by Ward, Bochner, and Furnham for a more in-depth discussion of culture shock. The content in this book is in no way intended to replace competent medical or psychological assistance, and readers are urged to consult with these professionals as appropriate.

Chapter Five:

Preparation for Success in the Cross-Cultural Sojourn

The first several chapters address culture, the transition process, and culture shock. While all of this can be interesting and helpful on its own, there are steps that you can take to help ease your experience of transitioning across cultures. This chapter includes eight suggestions for preparing for and navigating the transition well or helping someone else to navigate it well.

Big Idea #13:
Acknowledge your expectations

One of the things that has long baffled me about my college students comes up when I ask them about their expectations for their upcoming trip. Many of them say, "Well, I don't really have any." If I seem surprised, they say, "I'm trying to keep an open mind so I get the most out of the trip." Although this is a nice sentiment, it is simply not true that they have no expectations.

Everyone who engages in cross-cultural transitions has **expectations**. Businesspeople and missionaries are often at least more straightforward about their expectations than students tend to be. The better you do at acknowledging your expectations, the better you will do processing the cross-cultural transition. Here's why this is important: *many of your expectations will be frustrated.* If you acknowledge that certain goals are important to you, then you can recognize that they are not being met and respond to this as it happens. Otherwise, you will probably be left with a vague sense of unease and likely misattribute the cause to a relatively innocent source.

> James is a sales rep for a US manufacturer looking to do business overseas. Before leaving on his monthlong trip, his wife asks what his expectations are for the journey. He tells her, "I'm planning to make at least one big sale in each country I visit." She is supportive of his goals, and he sets off with this plan in mind.
>
> In the first country James visits, he meets his contact and begins discussing business on the way from the airport to the office. He doesn't get this sale and adjusts his tack with the next contact, waiting until his host brings up the business deal. Although he gets this sale, it isn't as big as he hoped for. With the third, fourth, and fifth businesses he interacts with, he is able to make a big sale, but he consistently feels like there is something he is missing in the interactions with the hosts.
>
> In the meantime, James is frustrated that his cell phone and credit card only work some of the time. After a week on the road, he gives up on trying to talk with his wife every day. After two weeks of travel, their conversations have grown increasingly short and tense, and he is frustrated that she can't understand what he's talking about.
>
> By the fourth week, James is ready to come home. Even though he has met his sales goal, he is sick of being on the road and is disappointed with the overall experience of traveling. The people he has been interacting with are friendly, but he doesn't really feel like he can trust them. At the same time, he's not sure how things will be with his wife, since they weren't able to talk for the last week because the internet was too slow for Skype, and his phone wasn't working anymore.

This brief story is intended to illustrate that James actually had a lot of expectations he didn't state before leaving. The sales goal was an expectation, but in spite of meeting it, he had an overall negative experience. Here are a few of his unstated expectations:

- James expected to be received as a competent professional. When his normal approaches to sales didn't work, he adjusted, but it was frustrating to him that he came across as incompetent.

- James expected to be able to develop rapport, and even a professional friendship, with some of his contacts. He expected to be able to do this in a way that was familiar to him, according to his normal patterns.

- James expected to be able to maintain good relations with his wife while traveling. He specifically expected to be able to talk with her at least four times a week though he never stated it as a goal. He also expected his wife to be able to understand what he was experiencing.

- James expected his technology and financial instruments to work without fail.

- James expected his return to be a happy one, without marital tension.

- James expected that he would really enjoy the trip and that this would be the first of many trips like it.

None of these expectations was unreasonable. However, it is unlikely that any or all of them would be fulfilled in the way that James expected. Of course, simply listing these expectations would not cause them to happen.

What creating a comprehensive and authentic assessment of expectations does accomplish is to make it possible to compare the actual experience to the expected experience. This in turn illuminates what might be causing frustrations and tensions during the sojourn. The best practice is to create an honest list of expectations before traveling, and to revisit it from time to time to see what did and did not come to fruition. Naturally, it may also be necessary to add to the list as new, formerly hidden, expectations come to light.

BIG IDEA #13 REFLECTION

(Preparation)

1. As you prepare for your sojourn, what expectations do you have? Try to list at least two in each relevant category:

    1) Professional / Career

    2) Academic

    3) Personal (health)

    4) Personal (self-improvement)

    5) Relational (co-nationals)

    6) Relational (hosts)

    7) Relational (back home)

    8) Spiritual (self)

    9) Spiritual (others)

    10) Service/Mission

    11) Support received (logistical, emotional, from Students International staff)

    12) Mentoring / training received (from Students International)

    13) Cultural/Linguistic (your own competence)

2. Revisit the list above, or if you did not make a list before beginning your trip go back and identify what expectations you had before beginning. How well have your expectations been met?

3. How many of your expectations have been frustrated?

4. How have you responded to success or frustration relative to your expectations?

(Return)

5. As you return, what expectations do you have? Try to list at least two in each relevant category:

   1) Professional / Career

   2) Academic

   3) Personal (health)

   4) Personal (self-improvement)

   5) Relational (co-workers)

   6) Relational (hosts that you are leaving behind)

   7) Relational (back home)

8) Spiritual (self)

9) Spiritual (others)

10) Service/Mission

11) Support received (logistical, emotional, from Students International staff)

12) Mentoring / training received (from Students International)

13) Cultural/Linguistic (your own competence)

6. Revisit the list above, or if you did not make a list before returning home from your trip go back and identify what expectations you had before returning. How well have your expectations been met?

7. How many of your expectations have been frustrated?

8. How have you responded to success or frustration relative to your expectations?

Big Idea #14:
Don't just be yourself

One of the more ill-conceived recommendations I have heard for a cross-cultural sojourner is this: "When you're over there, just be yourself!" Although the sentiment is a nice one, it is inappropriate for cross-cultural transitions. We define ourselves and our patterns in relation to our own culture, and when we import this cultural self into a host culture, there are elements that simply don't fit.

Think of it this way: within our own culture, we recognize that different behaviors are appropriate in different circumstances. The exuberance expressed at a football game is generally inappropriate for the workplace and vice versa. Yet both ranges of expression (football and office) can be part of who you are. The difference is that in the intercultural setting, you do not yet have the appropriate range of expression. Thus, whether you use your business self, your church self, or your party animal self, none of these personas are tuned to the demands of the cross-cultural setting. It is not appropriate to 'just be yourself,' any more than it is appropriate to act in a court of law as though it were a sports bar simply because you are your more accurate self when in a bar. Instead, you will probably need to adapt and expand what it means to be you when in a cross-cultural setting, just as you would when in an unfamiliar setting at home.

That said, it is important to recognize that there are certain elements of who you are that remain constant. If you are a husband or wife, or mother or father embarking on a trip, this does not change just because you are in a different culture. Travel is not license to disregard or lose sight of the permanent elements of who you are; however, they might have to be expressed differently in the culture you are visiting.

BIG IDEA #14 REFLECTION

(Preparation)

1. What are some situations that you have experienced at home where you have had to act differently in order to be appropriate to the situation?

2. Have you found it easy or difficult to learn appropriate norms for new situations?

3. From what you know about the host culture, what adaptations do you think you might have to make in order to be seen as acting appropriately there? What adaptations are you unwilling to make (for example, if something seems unethical to you)?

(Sojourn)

4. What elements of your personality have worked really well here – what have colleagues and hosts responded well to?

5. What have you had to change about how you present yourself here? Examples include clothing, volume, eye contact, directness, or indirectness of speech, etc.

(Return)

6. As you think back over your time away, what do you think are some of the biggest changes you ended up having to make about how you presented yourself?

7. What changes will you need to make in order to be appropriate now that you are returning?

Big Idea #15:
Learn to recognize the factors that intensify the experience

Most people I know have difficulty wrapping their heads around just why cross-cultural transitions can be so disruptive. Although we have already covered a number of those topics, this section presents another way to think about the disruption present in cross-cultural transition, using the idea of **intensity factors**. Michael Paige, one of the leading thinkers on international education, created a comprehensive list to explain what it is that makes intercultural experiences so intense.[22] I have adapted, expanded, and added to his ideas here.

- The more cultural difference that exists between the sojourner's host and home cultures, the more difficult the experience will be. In thinking about this idea, it is important to remember that cultures contain so many factors that it might be easy to underestimate the actual amount of difference. What's more, if you tend to view the differences as overly positive or negative, it can make the differences even more difficult to process, and thus more intense.

- In general, the less interculturally competent a person is, the more intense the experience will be.[23] Intercultural competence can be seen as a spectrum moving between mono-cultural (my culture is the only way) at one end and global (I understand my culture relative to other cultures) at the other. At the global end of the spectrum, people begin to develop the skill of frame shifting for the way they think and act so that they can move between cultures more naturally. The more people see their own culture as central to reality, the more intense the experience will probably be for them.

- Language plays a complicated role in increasing intensity in the cross-cultural sojourn. On the one hand, a lack of fluency in the host culture causes a significant increase in intensity because language is so important, not only in communicating ideas but also in the way that logic works.[24] On the other hand, at times the use of a good interpreter (who can translate not only words but ideas) may actually be a buffer against the real differences present between cultures, thus lowering the intensity of the experience. It is,

---

22 Paige, "On the Nature of Intercultural Experiences and Intercultural Education Chapter 1."
23 A possible exception to this is Bennett's developmental stage called *acceptance*, where difference is fairly well understood but ethical and epistemological commitments are still being developed in the more complex intercultural worldview.
24 Whorf, "Science and Linguistics."

after all, very disturbing to hear someone say something you understand linguistically but not logically or ontologically. Nonetheless, increased **linguistic competence** in general will lower the intensity of an experience.

- The degree to which you are immersed in the host culture also affects the cross-cultural intensity of the experience. If you tend to remain with other people from your own country and are able to utilize familiar-seeming hotels and restaurants, the experience will be less intense overall. However, these choices may at the same time create a significant barrier between you and your hosts, depending on the nature of your business. With some of the work I was involved with, we did not start making effective relational progress until we stayed in the homes of our hosts. This is of course more intense, but it was the most appropriate solution in that situation. Higher levels of immersion are generally more conducive to Students International's mission and vision. However, it can sometimes be useful to provide a respite from deep immersion to allow for processing. Immersion alone does not guarantee effective accomplishment of goals related to intercultural competence.[25]

- In general, possessing previous intercultural experience helps reduce the intensity of cross-cultural transitions. There are two caveats to this. First, it is possible to be present in a location without actually being present to the culture. Interculturalists sometimes refer to this phenomena as, for example, having an American experience in a Japanese location. In such a case, the prior experience would not actually be intercultural, and it would thus not reduce the intensity of the next experience. The second caveat flows from the first in that sometimes people assume they are better at crossing cultures than they actually are. For a person like this, like the student of mine I mentioned in the second chapter, a hard bout of culture shock can be deeply unsettling.

- One of the more complicated intensity factors relates to relative visibility. If a person is used to being a visible member of the majority group in their home culture (for example, being white in America), it can be difficult to suddenly be a visible minority (such as being white in sub-Saharan Africa). On the other hand, a person who is used to being a visible minority (such as being black in America) may find unsettling how their minority / majority experience is interpreted in the host culture. This happened to African American poet Langston Hughes, who was interpreted as being white while visiting Ghana, Africa. Thus, your own ethnic identity might be either unknown or misinterpreted while you are out of your home culture.

---

25 Paige, "The Georgetown Consortium Project: Interventions for Student Learning Abroad."

- Cross-cultural transitions can also bring about a change in perceived or relative status. For high school and college participants with Students International, this may take the form of reinterpreting themselves not as poor students but as relatively wealthy foreigners. That can be a very unsettling transition. On the other hand, you may find that your particular credential may not be recognized, thus lowering your status when visiting another country. For example, not everyone who is called "doctor" in the US could retain the title while in Germany, depending on where they have earned their degree. Even the label "college" can have varied meanings across cultures – sometimes meaning secondary education and elsewhere meaning university-level education. Such differences may seem insignificant until you find yourself trying to prove to someone that they are misinterpreting your relative status.

- One of the most frustrating intensity factors can be related to power and control. For Americans, who are used to a high degree of agency in taking care of themselves, it can be unnerving to play the role of guest. To be subject to the state bureaucracy, or even to be the recipients of the hospitality of another culture can be significantly frustrating for people unused to such things.

- I have also found[26] that team relationships, when a factor, can definitely increase the experience of intensity in the cross-cultural setting. Teams can be a great source of comfort and encouragement, but even normally functional teams can disintegrate and demonstrate unhealthy dysfunction under the stress generated by culture shock.

- Romance between the sojourner and anyone else is another intensity factor. Whether with a committed significant other at home, a team-member, a spouse traveling with you, or a member of the host culture, romantic relationships can absolutely increase the intensity of the sojourn. This is not to say that they need to be entirely avoided, but rather it should be understood that they are not neutral factors.

- The living environment is the final intensity factor.[27] This can take several forms, including climate, access to palatable food and beverage, access to medical care, and the presence of various threats like stinging or biting insects or animals and the presence and severity of unfamiliar diseases. I have seen situations where students were so focused on

---

26 Jones, "Intercultural Development in Global Service-Learning."
27 Ibid.

the living environment that they were unable to engage the culture meaningfully. Adequate preparation in this respect (without engendering paranoia) is very important for most sojourners.

- The spiritual climate is an additional intensity factor that can really change the nature of a cross-cultural sojourn – especially when you have ministry intent. This can include the spiritual health of yourself, the team, and the local church(es) along with the presence of other religions and outright spiritual opposition.

BIG IDEA #15 REFLECTION

(Preparation)

1. Review the list of intensity factors above. Which of these do you anticipate will increase the intensity of your sojourn and why?

(Sojourn)

2. Review the list of intensity factors above. Which of these have actually increased the intensity of your sojourn? How have they done so?

3. If you answered question 1 above, review the list of factors you expected to increase the intensity of your experience. What were you correct about? What factors have impacted you differently than you expected?

4. How has the intensity generated by these factors impacted your overall experience negatively and positively?

5. Spiritual battle is a very real intensity factor. Do you sense that there has been spiritual conflict related to your sojourn? What have you noticed in this regard? How have other Christians reacted or been involved?

6. Are there any steps you need to take regarding any of these intensity factors, or regarding your own spiritual health?

(Return)

7. Which of the intensity factors do you expect will impact your experience of re-turning home? Or, if you have already returned, which of the factors have impacted your return?

Big Idea #16:
Be aware of the factors that increase risk

In addition to the factors that increase intensity of cross-cultural sojourns, there are also a number of factors that can increase the risk people experience. These factors also make the experience potentially more difficult, and it is wise to be familiar with them so as to adequately prepare for and understand the experience. I also recommend regular (every two weeks or so) review of both the intensity factors and the risk factors to reflect on how they may be impacting your experience. This list is adapted and expanded from Paige's original conceptualization of the **risk factors**.[28]

- Different cultures have different boundaries for what is considered public and private, so elements of your life that ordinarily remain private may be brought out into the open or probed while on a sojourn, including financial and relational status. This may cause incredible discomfort. On the other hand, areas of your personal life that you want others to know might not be interesting or appropriate from the perspective of your hosts, thus introducing the risk of not being (or at least feeling) adequately known.

- Due to the difficulty that can be present in cross-cultural transitions, there is often a fairly high risk of failure. Depending on your (and Students International's, and/or your partner college's) threshold for failure, this possibility may be more or less acceptable. If possible, it is best to plan for a certain amount of failure and to create contingency plans. Failure can be particularly threatening to personality types that strive to be seen as successful, correct, or effective, or those who have a high need for affirmation.

---

28 Paige, "On the Nature of Intercultural Experiences and Intercultural Education Chapter 1."

- Embarrassment is a certainty while in cross-cultural transition. You will be embarrassed and you will embarrass and offend others. Plan for this, and do not be surprised when it happens. It can be difficult to know how to plan for contingencies, but it is a good idea to study up on how to make proper apologies in the culture where you are a guest. This information will also help you to recognize apologies if and when they come your way.

- Depending on how interculturally competent and culturally integrated you are at the beginning of your sojourn, you may find different kinds of threats to your cultural identity. In some cases, you may find that people reject certain elements of your culture that are very important to you. In other cases, you may find yourself rejecting your own culture. If you begin to identify with the host culture, you may also find yourself dealing with difficult issues about which culture you actually belong to. This issue is not limited to people on long-term transitions abroad. Even people on very short trips may find that if they have a sense of being alienated from their own culture it may be somehow inflamed by the travel.

- One of the most threatening risks that I have observed is that of **self-awareness**. On the one hand, self-awareness is an incredibly important skill for successful cross-cultural transitions. On the other hand, new awareness about oneself can be crippling in the short run. The risk of finding out how good you aren't at things you care about, for example, can be tremendously discouraging.

In my experience working with students abroad, the two most intense factors from this list and the previous list are team relations and#elf-awareness, with living environment a close third in some cases.

BIG IDEA #16 REFLECTION

(Preparation)

1. Review the list of risk factors above. Which of these do you anticipate will increase the difficulty of your sojourn and why?

2. Review the list of risk factors above. Which of these have actually increased the difficulty of your sojourn? How have they done so?

3. If you answered question 1 above, review the list of factors you expected to increase the risk in your experience. What were you correct about? What factors have impacted you differently than you expected?

4. How has the risk generated by these factors impacted your overall experience negatively and positively?

5. Are there any steps you need to take regarding any of these risk factors, or regarding your own spiritual health?

(Return)

6. Which of the risk factors do you expect will impact your experience of returning home? Or, if you have already returned, which of the factors have impacted your return?

Big Idea #17:
Prepare yourself to cope and be vigilant

In light of everything up to this point in this chapter, it would be understandable if you feel a little discouraged. The truth is that cross-cultural transitions are difficult, and their effect should not be underestimated. There is one more thing that we need to cover, and it is really important to your success in navigating (or helping someone else navigate) cross-cultural transitions: **coping.**

Given the psychological and physical stresses mentioned in this chapter, you need ways to cope with the stress. The reality is that *you will cope.* The question is how. I urge you to develop a coping plan before or early in the trip and to revisit it regularly. Healthy coping will enable you to continue to engage the culture and to accomplish the goals you set out to complete. Moreover, it will unlock the potential for long-term, high-quality friendships.

On the other hand, I feel compelled to issue a very stark warning: Unhealthy coping can absolutely undo you. Everyone has vices he or she is prone to. For some these are sexual; for some they are substance-related; for some they are financial, such as with gambling; for some they are relational or involve manipulation of or power over others; and for others these involve self-harm. There are, of course, many other vices, but you should not deceive yourself into imagining that you do not have your go-to vices. The reason that these may not be readily apparent to you is that most of us have created networks, points of contact, and relational support in our normal lives that reaffirm the better parts of who we are and that keep the worse parts of who we are in check.

In the cross-cultural transition, most of our sources of positive affirmation and moral guidance are suddenly absent. Not only that, but we find ourselves in a new cultural milieu with its own moral realities and complications. In such a setting, particularly when under stress, it can be easy to lose our moral bearings much more quickly than you might imagine possible.

For this reason, I highly recommend two action points. First, create a plan for how you can cope healthily. For example, allow yourself a certain amount of the comforts if they are available—movies, books, magazines, food, music—that keep you tied into home and comfort. Find creative outlets for stress, such as exercise, cooking, writing, or painting. You don't have to be particularly good at any of these things for them to help you. There are situations in which your normal coping mechanisms (running, for example) may not be available to you for cultural or safety reasons. Plan ahead on alternatives so that you are empowered to continue coping in a healthy way rather than being overwhelmed by this setback. It is good to find a mentor or coach who understands cross-cultural transitions who can help you process things when they get too deep.

The second action point is to regularly review the symptoms of culture shock listed in the previous chapter. When you start to recognize that you are exhibiting these symptoms, give yourself plenty of grace. At the same time, create healthy limits that will keep you from the worse outcomes of those symptoms. Also, watch for ways these might be playing out that you didn't expect. Physical aggressiveness, for example, will often come out in driving like an idiot rather than in punching someone. If you sense that you are getting in too deep, call a mentor.

One thing to be especially careful of is emotional dependency. There is a tendency present in many people, which can at times cross over into an actual psychological disorder, to overly attach yourself to another person, particularly in a time of intense stress. This feeling will often masquerade as love, but it tends to be very self-serving and often has characteristics of intense jealousy and possessiveness. This tendency can be very destructive, especially (but not only) in the event that it is at cross-purposes with the goal of your sojourn. Both in the emotional and sexual realms, this method of coping can have real and lasting negative consequences. A good mentor or psychologist can help you recognize and avoid these kinds of relationships and find alternative, healthier ways to cope.

BIG IDEA #17 REFLECTION

(Preparation)

1. Do you agree that coping will occur as you experience cross-cultural stress?

2. Do you have an experience of positive or negative coping to reflect on? If so, consider what you have learned from it.

3. Develop a coping plan for your time abroad. Remember that like many of your expectations this will have to be adjusted as you actually enact your sojourn.

4. What vices do you need to be particularly careful about?

(Sojourn)

5. Do you agree that coping has occurred as you experienced cross-cultural stress?

6. Do you have an experience of positive or negative coping to reflect on? If so, consider what you have learned from it.

7. Are there ways in which you have coped that you need to repent of or find healing from? Also, see Chapter Seven.

(Return)

8. As you prepare to return, are there ways in which you have coped that you need to deal with before going back. Are there mistakes or offenses you have made relationally or morally that you need to address?

9. How can you cope well on your return? Chapter Six will talk more about why this is necessary, but it is good to have a plan for coping as you return.

Big Idea #18:
Engage in constructive preparation

There are several really good ways to ready yourself for a cultural transition. Of course, one of the most important mechanisms for this is preparing yourself through increased self-awareness, as discussed earlier in this book. Another helpful kind of preparation is what I call *constructive preparation*. This kind of preparation involves becoming increasingly familiar with the culture you will be transitioning to prior to your departure. Here are a few ideas on how to do that:

- Watch movies and documentaries that take place in the culture you are visiting. You can also include the experiences of people from the place you are visiting while they themselves are abroad. If you are going to Nicaragua, you could watch movies that take place in Latin America as well as movies about Latin American people in the United States.

- Read travel guides, travelogues, and blogs from people who have gone before you. For culture-specific information, I especially recommend the Culture Shock series and anything published by Intercultural Press.

- Take a class about the country and the culture of the place you'll be going to.

- Check out books from the library. I especially recommend books with lots of pictures, as they help you imagine where you are going.

- If there is a mechanism to do this, try to meet people from the host culture before you go. For example, sometimes you can volunteer to help international students at local colleges and universities.

- Learn about the history of your host culture. Politics, religion, and economics are really useful in providing context.

As always, this list comes with a series of caveats. First, any media representation of the place you are going will be incomplete and often biased. That's okay as long as you recognize the limitation. Second, if you are able to make friends before you go, be aware that there may be expectations placed on you because of that relationship. For example, in some cultures friendship connections carry with them the expectation of financial assistance for the friend and his family. Importantly, this does not necessarily negate the validity of the friendship, as it may instead be a sign of the friendship. Nonetheless, being a friend may come with strings attached, and it is good to be aware upfront that this is possible.

BIG IDEA #18 REFLECTION

(Preparation)

1. How will preparing for a sojourn to another country differ from a trip to another part of your own country?

2. What do you expect to be the most helpful constructive preparation activity you can undertake before your trip?

(Sojourn)

3. How did preparing for a sojourn to another country differ from a trip to another part of your home country?

4. What was the most helpful activity you undertook before your trip?

5. If you have been gone for more than a couple of months, you might need to do some catching up on the culture back home. What do you think might be good preparation activities?

6. How will you prepare for a sojourn to another country in the future?

Big Idea #19:
Make friends

Once you arrive, it will serve you well to make friends in the host culture. A good host-culture friend will be able to serve as a guide and help you understand things that you aren't attuned to. A good host-culture friend will also be able to point out *faux pas* that you may be committing without realizing it.

If you don't already have a group of people around you from your own culture, it's also a good idea to make friends with a few expats, if they are available. People from your own country can give you pointers on how to navigate the local **bureaucracy**, the best places to eat, and what to avoid. They can also serve as a good outlet for commiserating about shared frustrations with the host culture.

Again, there are a couple of caveats in order here. First, when making friends across cultures, recognize that the first people most likely to engage in relationship with you are often themselves somewhat marginal in their own culture. People who are within the "normal" range of their own culture are often not particularly incentivized to reach out to foreigners. Those who do reach out to you may be doing so because you represent a way of thinking they find attractive, or because you are in some way exotic to them. This does not mean that you need to avoid these friendships, but it does mean that they can limit your ability to connect with non-marginal groups, so they must be considered carefully. If your role is particularly strategic, it might be worth pushing past the "low hanging" relational fruit and investing the hard work in developing relationships with more culturally central people.

A second thing about making friends with cultural hosts is that in some cultures, this will mean making friends with the whole family. You'll need to check the cultural norms in your area, but it would not be uncommon for you to be invited into family situations that would seem odd to bring a stranger into in your own culture. Again, not a big problem, but something to be aware of.

Finally, regarding expats, there are a couple of considerations. Beware the jaded expat. There are some who have such a negative attitude about the host culture (or their own culture) that it will be difficult for you to avoid being affected by this. Less damaging is the hopelessly optimistic expat, who refuses to take an honest look at the problems in the host culture, when of course such problems do exist. Also beware that in certain circumstances, affiliations with various people from your own culture can influence how your hosts interpret you.

BIG IDEA #19 REFLECTION

(Preparation)

1. How carefully do you choose friends now?

2. How might your methods of choosing friends change in your new environment?

3. What opportunities are available for you to make friends with host nationals? With expats?

(Sojourn)

4. What has worked well for you as you have sought to make new friends in the host country?

5. Do you need to develop a strategy to make additional friends?

6. Did you find that anyone wanting to become your friend was in some way marginal themselves?

7. What friendships are working out well, and which ones do you need to either put more energy into or consider dropping?

(Return)

8. What friendships do you want to continue when you return home?

9. Will you need to rekindle old friendships as you return home? Make new ones?

10. How has your approach to choosing and making friends changed now that you've returned?

Big Idea #20:
Have fun

This chapter has covered some of the realities that you should prepare for in the cross-cultural transition. While many of these concepts have a negative tone, crossing cultures can be one of the most rewarding and exciting human endeavors.

One of the best ways to have a successful cross-cultural experience is to have fun. Explore. Meet people. Ask questions. Be surprised. Be amazed. Record your sense of wonder. Collaborate. Embrace the experience. Enjoy the adventure. Innovate.

Cross-cultural transitions open your eyes to possibilities that you never could have seen—for yourself, for your business or cause, and for humanity. Engage the possibilities.

BIG IDEA #20 REFLECTION

(Preparation)

1. When have you made an effort to have fun in the past?

2. How might your methods for having fun change in your new environment?

3. Do you think there are new things that you might enjoy doing in your new environment?

(Sojourn)

4. What have you found to be really fun on your sojourn? List several activities and events that have been particularly enjoyable.

5. What fun things would you have never been able to do if you hadn't come here?

6. How have you replaced old forms of fun with new ones?

(Return)

7. How have your methods for having fun changed now that you've returned?

8. Are there kinds of fun that you will need to replace as you return?

9. Are there kinds of fun only available to you in your home country that you are looking forward tc experiencing again?

Chapter Six:
Coming Home and Welcoming Back

This chapter is intended to help you prepare for the process of coming home after a cross-cultural sojourn. If you yourself were not traveling, this chapter is also intended to help you welcome back a friend or loved one who has been traveling. Some of these items are redundant from the earlier chapters in the book, and you are encouraged to use this chapter as quick refresher as well as to go back into the earlier chapters and consider the topics in more depth. Depending on what stage of the sojourn you are in, you will find that the same material will strike you differently and generate new reflections.

Big Idea #21:
Coming home is transition all over again

For sojourners who have been gone for more than a couple of weeks (the exact amount of time will vary), the transition home follows essentially the same pattern as the transition abroad. There is a new set of endings, another neutral zone, and a new set of beginnings.

BIG IDEA #21 REFLECTION

(Return)

1. Do you accept the premise that returning home will most likely have the same pattern as transitions abroad? Why or why not?

2. As you reflect on the transition that you experienced coming here, do you expect that your transition will be easier or harder going back?

3. Go back to Chapter Three and complete the "return" reflection prompts. Then reflect on the experience of completing those prompts.

Big Idea #22:
Home just kind of . . . isn't

On returning home, culture shock will often play out again, although in this case, it is called **reentry shock**. Somewhat surprisingly, reentry shock is caused by basically the same tensions and realities that caused culture shock to begin with. Your mental map of how the world works has to flex back to fit the home culture. However, depending on how long you have been gone, the home culture has likely changed since you left.

The change to life back home is actually one of the most disturbing things about reentry shock. During a period of culture shock, many people (refugees excluded) have the reserve option to check out and return home. "No matter how bad it is here," you might reason, "I could go home and everything would be back to normal." The problem with this idea is twofold. First, as the sojourner, you may be indelibly changed by even a short experience. Thus, you are not the same "you" who left to embark on the sojourn. Second, home has changed. Your own culture has moved on in your absence, experiencing and processing realities that you might not have. This is true of family and friends, too. You have likely missed out on graduations, weddings, births, and deaths. Your family and friends have already finished processing information you might just be finding out about.

The cumulative effect is that on returning home, it doesn't feel quite like home. This can be far more disruptive than the initial culture shock. Because if home doesn't feel like home . . . what does?

BIG IDEA #22 REFLECTION

(Return)

1. Review Chapter Four and complete the return reflection prompts. Then reflect here on the experience of completing those prompts.

2. How or where do you most expect to notice that "home" will have changed during your absence?

3. Do you expect this experience to be unsettling? Why or why not?

4. Do you feel prepared to adjust to a new "normal" at home?

5. In what ways have you changed while gone?

6. Do you think others will recognize these changes in you, or do you think they will expect you to be the same as before?

Big Idea #23:
Do the transition well

Transitioning home can be done both well and poorly. Here are a few pointers for transitioning home well.

Before you leave the host culture:

- Process the new set of endings. What will no longer be true about you once you leave?

- Inasmuch as it is possible, reconcile any difficult relationships in the host culture. It is infinitely harder to accomplish this after leaving. Are there any relationships you need to reconcile?

- Make a list here of what you have experienced that really matters to you—you'll want to come back to this later.

- Write down the insights that the time in the host culture has given you. These might seem crystal clear at the moment, but they will get fuzzy after you leave.

- Make a list here of what you want to do if you come back to the host culture.

- It's not a bad idea to get pictures of friends, and don't forget about phone numbers. Write them down here – including some contextual information so you can recall why you wanted to remember them!

- Don't make promises you can't keep. It is often tempting to say, "I'll be back next year," or "I'll call you once a week." These might even seem reasonable at the moment, but they are generally unreasonable expectations. If you value the relationships you've developed, don't make unrealistic promises. This applies both to hosts and teammates.

Upon leaving the host culture, if you can avoid it, do not go straight home. For a trip of roughly six weeks or longer, I recommend a minimum of three to five full days in a third culture—a neutral location for a debrief. This is more important than most travelers realize, and it can be hard for many to justify the cost. However, this is one of the most important pieces of advice about the return home.

When you are in your host culture, there are some things that you will not be able to process because they are too close at hand. Not only that, but it can be hard to believe that you are really leaving. As soon as you arrive home, there are expectations (both your own and others') that make it difficult to process the immediate transition. Moreover, once you are home, it is too late to prepare to go home! So what to do while in the third location?

- Rest and relaxation. This is a serious recommendation and is not in the least bit frivolous. Returning home rested will greatly improve the first week of transition.

- Map out what has happened during your sojourn. Make a month-by-month map of your social, cultural, academic, and spiritual well-being from their sojourn. Give each topic its own color of ink or some kind of a key, draw your map here. Mark significant moments of change with words of explanation.

- Look through the headlines of news and movies that came out in the last several months, so you have some sense of what people are talking about upon your return. Write down some of the highlights here

- Create an **elevator speech** in which you can describe your experience in 30 seconds or less. Although many people will express interest, few (at least in American culture) are interested in hearing more than about a minute of your experience. Creating a couple of concise explanations of your experience will allow you to share something of meaning in a way that lets you play it safe.

Sample Elevator Speech

Friend: How was your trip? I want to hear all about it!
Response: I really learned a lot! I was gone for six months and was able to spend time in Africa and France. I was surprised by how good and how hard it was, but I made some great friends. One of the most surprising things I learned was all the different ways that people can see the world!
Friend: Sounds fascinating! I'd love to see pictures sometime. Gotta run—see you later!

Write your elevator speech(es) here:

- Prepare yourself for disappointment. The reality is that many of your friends and family will not understand what a life-changing, challenging, or wonderful sojourn you have been on. Even more disappointing, depending on how long you have been gone, there may actually be people who ask you when you are going to leave on the trip—even if you've been out of the country for six months or more!

- Develop a list of expectations for your return home. Just like the trip abroad, the more honest you are about the expectations you have for going home, the better you will be able to process what happens. Many people have "scripts" that play in their heads about what it will be like to be welcomed home. These are rarely fulfilled in real life. If you are honest about what you are expecting, it will make it easier to assign disappointment where it belongs and move on. Revisit Big Idea 13 to complete this list. Then reflect on your expectations here:

- Create an honest list of disappointments and joys that you experienced during your sojourn. This is just for yourself, so make it really honest.

- Create another list of insights gained now that you've exited the host culture.

- Revisit Chapter Five and create a list of goals, coping mechanisms, and next steps for your return. This is the last moment of clarity you might have for several months. Use it!

1. Goals:

2. Coping Mechanisms:

3. Next Steps:

- If you have coped in unhealthy ways, are there things you need to do to make this right? Do you need to seek forgiveness? Remember 1 John 1:9 *But if we confess our sins to God, he can always be trusted to forgive us and take our sins away.* If you need to confess and repent, use this space to make a plan to do that. Who will you talk with? When? About what?

- Because you will be spending a lot of energy on all of this mental processing, be sure to take time to have a little fun and laugh. This is not frivolity, either—you need to balance out your energy with some fun. Be a tourist. You are not in this third culture to engage that culture—it's just a stopover point. Go to a museum, enjoy a park, or visit a landmark.

Upon your actual return to your home culture, anticipate that you will likely experience the stages of culture shock again as you move through reentry shock. For many people, there is an initial euphoria that sets in, although this will often quickly give way to irritability and hostility as people try to relate to the person you were before, rather than the person you are now. If you are welcoming someone back, give them room to express themselves, but don't push for too many details right away.

Coming home is somewhat like walking from a lighted room into a dark room or vice versa—it takes a little time to adjust before you can function. I do not recommend keeping a very ambitious schedule in the first few weeks after returning home, but it is important not to just retreat into your house or room. Here are a few things to expect:

- The intensity and risk factors will again be at play, but differently. For example, thinking of visibility and invisibility, a Peace Corps worker who has become accustomed to being a visible minority in their country of service might have trouble adjusting to the relative anonymity of "fitting in" back home.

- The process of reentry shock is, in my experience, often slightly longer than the experience of culture shock. Moreover, the low is often a little bit lower than it was during culture shock. This means that the feelings of depression and discouragement will again be present. If you continue to process through the experience, this lowness will again be transitory. Six months is not at all unusual for the process of reentry.

- Don't skip the processing! It is very tempting to do whatever it takes to reassimilate into your home culture, but a failure to adequately process through reentry can cause long-term issues that will crop up at unexpected times. If you need to function at a very high level during this time and find yourself unable to do so, it may be worth consulting a medical professional. Again, this is almost always a transitory issue, so even though you may exhibit depression-like symptoms, it does not mean that you are clinically depressed. However, short-circuiting the processing can lead to adjustment disorder, as mentioned previously.

- Watch out for **shoeboxing**, an idea that originated with Bruce LaBrack, who is one of the leading advocates of reentry training.[29] Essentially, the idea is that it may be tempting to say, "Oh, wasn't that a nice trip," and put all of your memories, souvenirs, pictures, and so on, in a literal or figurative shoebox and set them off to the side. This allows you to revisit them at your leisure, but it does not allow the experience to be reintegrated into your long-term vision of life.

- Be intentional about coping. Just as in culture shock, the reentry transition can give rise to unhealthy coping mechanisms. Excessive busyness, crazy driving, excessive shopping, misuse of sexuality or relationships, and withdrawal are some of the most common unhealthy coping mechanisms I have seen used. A healthy coping plan and supports will help you avoid causing long-term problems.

- If possible, link in with a support network. If you were on the sojourn with a team, attempt to meet at least once every week for the first six months or so to debrief and catch up with each other. I have seen a real difference between sojourners who have done this and those who haven't. Those who do fare much better. It is also important to use this time to process unresolved relational tensions from the team, if these exist.

- Revisit the question of intercultural competence. I suggest taking the Intercultural Development Inventory and the Intercultural Effectiveness Scale about six months after returning.[30] Taking them earlier than that will often give you results that relate to your transition rather than to your more stable underlying orientations to difference and similarity. Go over these with a coach, consultant, or mentor, and process your experience again.

I have observed that beyond the initial reentry shock, there is also a stage of reintegration.[31] This stage can last for several months or even years beyond the initial struggle of reentry, and it involves the quest to integrate lessons learned into your business, education, or cause. This is an

---

29 http://www2.pacific.edu/sis/culture/

30 For information on taking these instruments, contact us at www.iamintercultural.com

31 Kiely, "A Chameleon with a Complex: Searching for Transformation in International Service-Learning."

important goal, and it is worth reflecting on from time to time to gauge progress.

As friends and family who are welcoming a loved one back from a cross-cultural sojourn, it can be very disconcerting to see the struggles that he or she is going through. Be patient. The worst of culture and reentry shock are almost always transitory. Listen. One of the most important things the sojourner needs is a supportive audience. Don't be surprised if you don't understand everything that he or she is talking about or if some of the ideas seem radical to you. This is often just part of the process of trying to figure out what fits where.

BIG IDEA #23 REFLECTION

(Preparation)

1. If you read this section while preparing to go abroad, how realistic does it seem to you that you will encounter some kind of transitional difficulty (reentry shock) when you come back home?

(Sojourn)

2. Do you think you will struggle with reentry as you go home? Are there any pointers in this section that might cause you to treat your experience differently now?

3. Look back over the list of symptoms of culture shock in pages 54-59. Do you recognize any of these symptoms at play in your life now? If so, which ones?

3. What three key items do you expect to find most valuable in Big Idea #23? Why?

    1)

    2)

    3)

4. How do you plan to accomplish these?

(Return)

5. How successful was your plan to accomplish these?

6. Look back over the list of symptoms of culture shock in pages 68-73. Do you recognize any of these symptoms at play in your life now? If so, which ones?

7. If you have been home for a while, has this list changed since you first returned home? How?

Chapter Seven:
Concluding Thoughts

Big Idea #24:
Transition is hard...even for Christians

Transitioning across cultures is an important part of fulfilling the mission of Students International:

Bringing students and the poor together cross-culturally
to encounter God, share the Good News, disciple and serve others in
occupational ministries.

It may seem that with such a purpose that Students International staff and participants should somehow be exempted from the rigors of cross-cultural transition. Yet following Jesus across cultures does not remove or reduce the difficulties found in transition. Indeed the toll of living a life of mission is a heavy one: "Make no mistake about it: obeying the Lord's command to disciple the nations has and always will be costly. It is risky business."[1] Indeed, a whole field of support services for missionaries has grown up around the particular needs of Jesus followers whose lives take them into cross-cultural and international living as His representatives.[2]

What we find is that rather than being exempted from the rigors of culture shock, participants and staff at organizations like Students International may even have additional pressures when crossing cultures. This can come from several sources. One is the tendency for other church people to look at Students International people as 'more spiritual' and to elevate them as a better sort of Christian. This produces an inaccurate and unhelpful pressure that suggests that you are not supposed to struggle with the same things that every other Christian struggles with while at the same time increasing the pressure on you to "produce" things that Christians care about. The problem is that these human pressures are not accurate reflections of what it looks like to

---

1 O'Donnell, *Missionary Care*, 1.

2 Member Care Associates, Mission Training International, Missionary Care Services, Minnesota Renewal Center, Barnabas International and other organizations exist for this purpose. The volume by O'Donnell (*Doing Member Care Well.*) has a more complete, though somewhat outdated list.

live with, follow, and be transformed by Christ.

At the same time, unfortunately, many times in Christian organizations there are also pressures 'on the field' with poor relationships between staff and other staff, Christian host-nationals, team members (of various backgrounds), home-office staff, and other host nationals. Hiebert once observed that missionaries have a tendency to under-support one another as they transition to the field:

> *Caught unaware, we are unable to cope with the problems of living in a new culture. We are overwhelmed by constantly having to face confusing situations and the strain of learning a new way of life. There is little time for leisure—after all, is it proper for missionaries to relax when there is so much to do? Our support systems are gone. We are part of a mission-ary community made up of strong-willed strangers to whom we do not dare admit weakness, and there may be no one to pastor us when we fail.[3]*

The reality of the endeavor that you are part of is that it is very difficult. When people let you down, it is important to acknowledge it, and to mourn the unfulfilled expectations. When you are wrestling with Christ, it is important that you wrestle honestly with Him. Take heart in the wrestling of Paul in Romans 7, who cries out that he does what he does not want to do and does not do what he wants to – he likens his struggle to a war within himself. This is powerful language of struggle. At the end of the chapter he calls out "**Wretched man that I am! Who will deliver me from this body of death?**" The answer immediately follows "**Thanks be to God through Jesus Christ our Lord!**" (Romans 7:24-25 ESV)

You might struggle mightily as you transition across cultures. Do not be surprised by this. Take heart that Jesus himself anticipated the struggles of those who would follow Him "**I have told you this, so that you might have peace in your hearts because of me. While you are in the world, you will have to suffer. But cheer up! I have defeated the world.**" (John 16:33). Consider the following verses of encouragement as we seek to locate ourselves in the journey of following Christ Across Cultures:

Romans 8:37

In everything we have won more than a victory because of Christ who loves us.

---

3 Hiebert, *Anthropological Insights for Missionaries*, 73.

2 Corinthians 2:14

I am grateful that God always makes it possible for Christ to lead us to victory. God also helps us spread the knowledge about Christ everywhere, and this knowledge is like the smell of perfume.

2 Corinthians 4:7

We are like clay jars in which this treasure is stored. The real power comes from God and not from us.

2 Corinthians 6:4

But in everything and in every way we show we truly are God's servants. We have always been patient, though we have had a lot of trouble, suffering, and hard times.

BIG IDEA #24 REFLECTION

Capture your thoughts after reflecting on the scripture selections above.

(Preparation)

(Sojourn)

Parting Words

Whether you are preparing for your first trip abroad or are a seasoned traveler, I hope you have found this guide to be a useful companion. The opportunity to cross cultures can be a great privilege. I urge you to make the most of it by taking the concepts in this book seriously. A few thoughts for specific groups follow.

Students Studying Abroad and Global Service-Learners

Make the most of your trip by setting intentional goals. One of the biggest limitations you may face is that you will tend to interact only with people from your socioeconomic class. Make an effort to get out into the community and get to know people and their stories. Host family stays are wonderful, but they are most effective when there are a few other people from your own culture that you can interact with. Don't avoid all contact with people who are like you, and at the same time, make sure you have some contact with people who are different from you. One of the biggest temptations you might face is to simply treat this experience as a resume builder. Be intentional and take the opportunity to develop into a more capable and creative adult.

One of the most challenging things that you will likely face is the difficulty in reintegrating what you have been learning with life back home. You, more than many others, will likely find reentry and reintegration to be an incredibly trying time. You want to make a difference, and whether or not you have become disillusioned, you are going to find it discouraging that few others understand your perspective on the world. Hang on and journal a lot, because you have a lot to offer the world. At the same time, watch out for the tendency to judge your own culture as particularly bad compared to other cultures (this is called reversal). If you sense this tendency (it is often accompanied by a kind of self-righteous overattachment to another culture), seek out

134

someone who can help you take the Intercultural Development Inventory and process through this. Of course reversal is not limited to these travelers, and every sojourner would do well to watch out for this.

Students International Staff

Slow down. Refuse to live at such a hectic pace that you do not allow yourself room to process. It is not a sign of spiritual weakness to encounter culture shock. It is, instead, a sign that you are human. Practice grace with yourself, your family, and those around you. Pushing through the difficulties of culture shock, although an admirable goal, is foolish. Take the time to process it. Don't think that you won't be faced with your own weakness and darkness. You will. The more you can accept the reality that you need grace, too, the more effective you will be.

Trailing Spouses and Third-Culture Kids

If you find yourself "along for the ride," your transition may be more difficult than your spouse's or parent's, as his or her time will generally be more structured than yours. Be intentional about

figure out where you're from and how to fit in. As a family, take time to recognize the effects that the cultural transition is having on you. The strain can be significant, so be sure to reaffirm your commitment to each other as part of your coping process.

Family and Friends of Sojourners

If you have read this book as a family member or friend of someone going through transition, several pieces of advice. First, be available. Second, don't be surprised if the sojourner you are supporting doesn't act like they need you or want to talk as often as you thought they might. Third, when the person going through transition tells you that everything is horrible, take it with a grain of salt. Often, you are the safest person they can talk to, and simply verbalizing their frustration is precisely what they need to make it better. Resist the temptation to overreach, but remain a constant presence. Don't be too nosy, but don't be absent. It's a bit of a balancing act, but in the long run, your presence and willingness to listen is what is most valuable.

Sponsors of Various Sojourns

If you are a study abroad adviser or program director, are Students International Staff, work in the home office, or in some other way are involved with sending people into cross-cultural sojourns, in many ways this book was written for you. You are responsible for the healthy transition of those you send across cultures. You must adequately prepare them for and support them during their sojourn. I emphatically add that you have a moral responsibility to ensure that the sojourner receives adequate reentry support and training upon their return. This is your responsibility—do not shirk it.

I have enjoyed this small journey with you, and I hope that you have found this resource to be a helpful one.

Bon voyage!

References

Bennett, Milton J. "A Developmental Approach to Training for Intercultural Sensitivity." *International Journal of Intercultural Relations*, Special Issue: Theories and Methods in Cross-Cultural Orientation, 10, no. 2 (1986): 179–96. doi:10.1016/0147-1767(86)90005-2.

———. *Basic Concepts of Intercultural Communication: Paradigms, Principles, & Practice: Selected Readings.* Second Edition. Boston: Intercultural Press, A Nicholas Brealey Pub. Company, 2013.

———. *Basic Concepts of Intercultural Communication: Selected Readings.* Nicholas Brealey Publishing, 1998.

Bridges, William. *Transitions: Making Sense of Life's Changes, Revised 25th Anniversary Edition.* 2 Exp Upd. Da Capo Press, 2004.

Clayton, Patti H. "Generating, Deepening, and Documenting Learning: The Power of Critical Reflection in Applied Learning." In *Teaching and Learning through Critical Reflection*, 1–26, n.d.

Condon, John C., and Bruce LaBrack. "Culture, Definition of." Edited by Janet Marie Bennett. *The SAGE Encyclopedia of Intercultural Competence.* A Sage Reference Publication. Los Angeles: SAGE Publications, Inc, 2015.

Condon, John C, and Fathi S Yousef. *An Introduction to Intercultural Communication.* Indianapolis: Bobbs-Merrill, 1974.

Hesselgrave, David J. *Communicating Christ Cross-Culturally, Second Edition.* 2 Sub. Zondervan, 1991.

Hiebert, Paul G. *Anthropological Insights for Missionaries.* Baker Academic, 1986.

Hoffman, Eva. *Lost in Translation: A Life in a New Language.* Penguin (Non-Classics), 1990.

Jones, Stephen W. "Intercultural Development in Global Service-Learning." Master's Thesis, University of the Pacific, 2011. http://www.amazon.com/Intercultural-Development-Global-Service-Learning-Stephen/dp/1489501207/.

Kiely, Richard C. "A Chameleon with a Complex: Searching for Transformation in International Service-Learning." *Michigan Journal of Community Service Learning* Spring 2004 (n.d.).

Kluckhohn, Florence (Rockwood), and Fred L. Strodtbeck. *Variations in Value Orientations.* Evanston, Ill.: Row, Peterson, and Company, 1961.

Kohls, L. Robert. *Survival Kit for Overseas Living: For Americans Planning to Live and Work Abroad.* 4th ed. London: Published by Nicholas Brealey Pub. in association with Intercultural Press, Yarmouth, Maine, 2001.

Lingenfelter, Sherwood G., and Marvin K. Mayers. "God's Metaphor for Ministry: The Incarnation." In *Ministering Cross-Culturally: An Incarnational Model for Personal Relationships*, 2nd ed., 12–25. Baker Academic, 2003.

Lucas, John. "Over-Stressed, Overwhelmed, and Over Here: Resident Directors and the Challenges of Student Mental Health Abroad." *Frontiers: The Interdisciplinary Journal of Study Abroad* XVIII (Fall 2009): 187–216.

Mayers, Marvin K., and Sherwood G. Lingenfelter. *Ministering Cross-Culturally: An Incarnational Model for Personal Relationships.* 2nd ed. Baker Academic, 2003.

Oberg, Kalervo. "Cultural Shock: Adjustment to New Cultural Environments." *Curare* 29, no. 2 (1960 2006): 3.

O'Donnell, Kelly. *Doing Member Care Well: Perspectives and Practices from around the World*. William Carey Library, 2002.

O'Donnell, Kelly S., ed. *Missionary Care: Counting the Cost for World Evangelization*. Pasadena, Calif: W. Carey Library, 1992.

Paige, R. Michael. "On the Nature of Intercultural Experiences and Intercultural Education Chapter 1." In *Education for the Intercultural Experience*, 2nd ed., 1–19. Intercultural Press, 1993.

———. "The Georgetown Consortium Project: Interventions for Student Learning Abroad." *Frontiers: The Interdisciplinary Journal of Study Abroad* XVIII (Fall 2009): v-75.

Pollock, David C., and Ruth E. Van Reken. *Third Culture Kids: Growing up among Worlds*. Rev. ed. Boston: Nicholas Brealey Pub, 2009.

Schaetti, Barbara F. "Global Nomad, Third Culture Kid, Adult Third Culture Kid, Third Culture Adult: What Do They All Mean?" *Families in Global Transition*. Accessed January 3, 2017. http://www.figt.org/global_nomads.

Storti, Craig. *The Art of Coming Home*. Nachdr. Yarmouth, Me: Intercultural Press, 2003.

———. *The Art of Crossing Cultures*. 2. ed. Boston, Mass., London: Nicholas Brealey Publ, 2007.

Ting-Toomey, Stella. *Communicating across Cultures*. The Guilford Communication Series. New York: Guilford Press, 1999.

Trompenaars, Fons. *Riding the Waves of Culture: Understanding Diversity in Global Business*. Burr Ridge, Ill: Irwin Professional Pub, 1994.

Ward, Colleen, Stephen Bochner, and Adrian Furnham. *Psychology Culture Shock - Ed2*. 2nd ed. Routledge, 2001.

Whorf, Benjamin L. "Science and Linguistics." In *Basic Concepts of Intercultural Communication: Selected Readings*, edited by Milton J. Bennett, 85–95. Nicholas Brealey Publishing, 1998.

Glossary

ambivalence: an inability to make decisions, wherein multiple options seem equally possible or equally disinteresting.

apathy: a sense of not caring, often accompanied by an inability to engage one's environment, even to his or her own detriment.

bureaucracy: the official systems that an organization or government uses to accomplish its business. In the international setting, bureaucracy is usually confusing to people from other cultures (and sometimes to people who live there as well). The process of navigating a bureaucracy to accomplish something like renewing a visa or paying your power bill can be very frustrating, especially in countries without a high value on efficiency.

coping: refers to the way in which people try to deal with difficult circumstances. Sometimes people cope by removing the difficulty, or by removing themselves from the situation in which the difficulty is occurring. However, it is often not possible to completely escape the stressor, which in turn requires people to develop ways to deal with the ongoing stress. Some of these ways are healthy, or adaptive, while others are destructive, or maladaptive.

culture shock: the effects of cumulative disorientation that comes from extended contact with another culture, often proceeding in three stages: emotional high, disenchantment / discouragement, and developing confidence.

culture: According to Milton Bennett, culture is the learned and shared values, beliefs, and behaviors of a group of interacting people. More simply, culture is "how people do their stuff together."

cumulative disorientation: the primary cause of culture shock, the result of extended exposure to another culture, in which a person's 'map' of how the world works is repeatedly violated by the host culture.

disenchantment: the stage of culture shock during which a sojourner discovers that the host culture and the experience overall are not as fun or positive as they originally seemed. This is often accompanied by a growing realization of the sojourner's own ineptitude in the host culture.

disintegration: a growing incapacity to function. This can look like having trouble getting out of bed, difficulty relating to coworkers, inability to accomplish tasks, or even unusual outbursts of emotion. Often the most distressing thing about disintegration is that you discover that something you were once good at is now extremely difficult. This is almost always a passing stage, but it is deeply disturbing.

elevator speech: a short (often 30 seconds or less) summary of your experience, designed to gauge how interested your listener is in finding out more about your experience. It should be concise enough that you could share the entire speech during an elevator ride.

illogical enjoyment of the host culture, and tends to interpret the world (especially the host

emotional high: often the first stage of culture shock, in which a person experiences an often illogical enjoyment of the host culture, and tends to interpret the world (especially the host culture) through an overwhelmingly positive lens.

endings: the first stage of transition, in which things which were once true about a person are no longer true or applicable due to the transition.

expat: someone who is living out of his or her home country (also called *passport country*) for an extended period of time.

expectations: the often unstated assumptions about what will (or what should) happen. While expectations are not bad, they are most helpful when they are acknowledged, because they often will not be fulfilled, or at least not in the ways you anticipate.

frame shifting: the capacity to move back and forth between one's own cultural reference set (cognitive and/or behavioral) and another culture's reference set.

global nomad: a person who for one reason or another does not have a permanent home, and who generally lives in one country only for a few years at a time before moving on. For a few, this is a lifestyle choice. For some this is the reality required by the profession the person is in. This can lead to a sense of being a global citizen on the one hand, and to a sense of rootlessness on the other.

global: referring to a way of seeing the world that acknowledges that there are many different perspectives. While this idea does not require that you agree with other perspectives, it does imply that you understand that these perspectives make sense to the people that hold them. For example, you might not agree with indirect communication as the best way to communicate, but with a global mindset you are able to understand that some people have really legitimate reasons for thinking that it is the best way to communicate.

homesickness: an experience of profoundly missing one's home, especially family and friends. Homesickness is not limited to cultural transitions, but is often especially profound when the ability to return home is further limited by geographic distance.

honeymoon stage: the honeymoon stage is another way to describe the "emotional high" at the beginning of culture shock.

intensity factors: the features of a cross-cultural experience that make it more difficult, especially psychologically.

intercultural competence: can be used to refer to various measures of how effective a person is at functioning across cultures. One of the most important ways to define intercultural competence is in relation to a person's ability to accurately understand and relate to both cultural difference and cultural similarity – a mode of competence that is measured by the Intercultural Development Inventory. Other measures of intercultural competence focus on resiliency, adaptation, and similar interactions between a person and his/her social and physical environments.

jet lag: extreme tiredness cause by travel, such as by airplane, and especially by rapidly changing multiple time zones. This is especially pronounced when 'flipping' the day and night as a result of literally being on the other side of the world. The effects of jet lag can last more than a week, and can cause impaired judgement.

journaling: a process used for recording one's experiences and thoughts. Especially useful for critical reflection. Blogging also can be useful, although for many people a physical journal seems to be more useful for sorting out difficult personal issues brought to the fore by transitions.

linguistic competence: refers to the ability to accurately understand and communicate in a language, especially including listening, speaking, reading, and writing. There are various measures of linguistic competence, but it has been estimated that it takes ten years to become fluent in a target language, meaning that there are no significant gaps (especially in expressions and specialized vocabulary).

monocultural: held in contrast to *global*, a person with a monocultural mindset can only acknowledge his or her own culture's perspective on the way the world works. Not only is the person's culture the right way to understand the world, it's really the only way.

neutral zone: see 'transition zone'.

new beginnings: the final stage of transition, in which a person's identity begins to reorganize and incorporate new elements which were not previously experienced.

reentry shock: refers to the intense psychological discomfort that accompanies returning home after a significant cross-cultural experience. This is very similar to culture shock, and often follows the same pattern, although it can last longer and can even be more difficult than culture shock.

risk factors: the elements of an experience that increase the feeling of risk, especially psychologically.

self-awareness: the extent to which you recognize how you function and how you are perceived by others. One the one hand, self-awareness is a very useful trait for success across cultures. On the other hand, it can be uncomfortable to realize how you come across. Additionally, an extreme self-awareness can keep you from actually engaging with other people and can thus be debilitating.

shoeboxing: packing up all of your memories associated with a cross-cultural sojourn in to a literal or metaphorical shoebox, only accessing them from time to time. This is held in contrast to integrating lessons and insights from the sojourn into your life.

sojourner(s): a person who is away from home, generally in another country, and often with some purpose for their travel, such as business, study, or exploration.

tacit knowledge: the things that we know without having to acknowledge that we know them – the knowledge in the back of our minds.

third-culture kid: A third-culture kid grows up in a culture which is neither his nor that of his parents. At the same time, he is not a member of the host culture. Thus, he is in between his home (or passport) culture, and his host (or adoptive culture). Because he is not a member of either culture, he is called a 'third-culture' kid. Common examples are missionary kids, military brats, and diplomat's kids.

thread of continuity: those elements of a person which remain constant before, during, and after a transition, even if they are not necessarily experienced as constant by the person undergoing transition.

transition zone: the middle stage of a transition, during which a person's identity is particularly challenged by the transition. It is often difficult to gain traction during this time. Also called the neutral zone.

Appendix:
Culture Shock and Mental Health

Some scholarly articles have been written about the connection between mental health and cultural transitions. For study abroad, I specifically recommend:

Lucas, John. (Fall, 2009). "Over-stressed, overwhelmed, and over here: Resident directors and the challenges of student mental health abroad." *Frontiers: The interdisciplinary journal of study abroad.* XVIII. Available online at:

http://frontiersjournal.org/wp-content/uploads/2015/09/LUCAS-FrontiersXVIII-Overstres
sedOverwhelmedandOverHere.pdf

To find out more about adjustment disorder, talk with a mental health professional. You can also find out more about this topic from the *Diagnostic and Statistical Manual of Mental Disorders.* Version 5 (2013) is available at www.dsm5.org

ABOUT THE AUTHOR

Stephen W. Jones is Assistant Professor of International Studies at Crown College in St. Bonifacius, MN. He holds a Master of Arts in Intercultural Relations from the University of the Pacific (Stockton, CA) in conjunction with the Intercultural Communication Institute (Portland, OR). He also has a B.A. in Bible and Intercultural Studies and a B.S. in Business Administration: Intercultural Management from Grace University (Omaha, NE).

Jones's introduction to teaching in the field of intercultural studies came when he delivered an intensive Cultural Anthropology course for an American university in Mali, West Africa in 2007. He has worked with groups involved in overseas study and service in Africa, Europe, Latin America, and Asia, as well as in various subcultures of the United States. In 2009 he began to directly manage the programming; curriculum; course development; and preparatory, on-site, and return teaching for students who were studying on five to six month intercultural immersion trips.

In 2012 he was also responsible for overseeing a team of students who were in Mali, West Africa when that country experienced a coup d'état, and he went to great lengths to assure a successful return home for those students. Jones has rich personal experience in various cultural settings and in industries ranging from agriculture to hospitality to higher education to financial services.

Jones is the author of "Transitions Across Cultures" and "Intercultural Development of Global Service-Learning." He is an Interculturalist who has worked with applied learning, service-learning, and/or community development in rural Nebraska; Mali, West Africa; urban Mississippi; Seattle, Washington; Omaha, Nebraska; and Minneapolis, Minnesota. He is especially interested in the intersection between racial/ethnic reconciliation, community development (international & domestic), and intercultural competence.

Jones has rich personal experience in many different cultural settings and industries. Among other lines of work, he has worked variously as a ranch hand at a cow-calf operation, in the hospitality industry, as a youth leader for an urban scouting program, as an accounting analyst in the financial services industry, as an AmeriCorps VISTA, and as higher education staff and faculty.   http://www.iamintercultural.com

Photo and Illustration Credits

1.	Front Cover Sunset	Florida	2014	Rose Marie Potras
2.	Flyleaf Mountain Boat	Fiji	2014	Stephen W. Jones
3.	Page 3 Students International	Logo		Students International
4.	Page 4 Plane	Atlanta	2016	Stephen W. Jones
5.	Page 12 Sky wing	Airborne	2016	Stephen W. Jones
6.	Page 18 Wood weave	Fiji	2014	Stephen W. Jones
7.	Page 24 Stoplight	Illustration	2013	Philip McBride
8.	Page 28 Highway	Airborne	2015	Stephen W. Jones
9.	Page 34 Map	Illustration	2013	www.fruitful-design.com
10.	Page 38 Green Boat Dock	Maine	2016	Rose Marie Potras
11.	Page 46 Road	Maine	2016	John H. Jones
12.	Page 56 Yarn	Fiji	2014	Stephen W. Jones
13.	Page 58 Transitions	Illustration	2013	Philip McBride
14.	Page 62 Village Street	Guatemala	2015	Stephen W. Jones
15.	Page 65 Slime	Minnesota	2016	Rose Marie Potras
16.	Page 69 Surf Crash	California	2016	Rose Marie Potras
17.	Page 73 Culture Shock	Illustration	2013	Philip McBride
18.	Page 77 Volcano	Guatemala	2015	Stephen W. Jones
19.	Page 82 Village Town	Guatemala	2015	Stephen W. Jones
20.	Page 88 Reflection	Virginia	2016	John H. Jones
21.	Page 96 Potomac Falls	Virginia	2016	Rose Marie Potras
22.	Page 98 Window	Guatemala	2015	Stephen W. Jones
23.	Page 102 Lighthouse	Michigan	2016	Rose Marie Potras
24.	Page 114 Orange Sky	Airborne	2016	Stephen W. Jones
25.	Page 126 Tree Palm Chairs	Fiji	2014	Stephen W. Jones
26.	Page 130 Sun Palm Trees	Fiji	2014	Stephen W. Jones
27.	Page 135 Cows	Guatemala	2015	Stephen W. Jones
28.	Page 136-137 Path Bikers	Massachusetts	2016	Rose Marie Potras
29.	Page 146 Stephen W. Jones	Nebraska	2016	Rose Marie Potras
30.	Flyleaf Mountain Ocean	Fiji	2014	Stephen W. Jones
31.	Back Cover Sunset	Florida	2014	Rose Marie Potras

Additional Notes

Additional Notes

Additional Notes

CPSIA information can be obtained
at www.ICGtesting.com
Printed in the USA
LVHW071915060819
626770LV00001B/1/P

9 781940 105048